QR코드를 촬영하면 원어민 음성파일
다운로드 페이지로 이동합니다.

같은 생각 다른 표현 스몰토크 편

초판1쇄 인쇄·2025년 6월 11일
초판1쇄 발행·2025년 6월 11일

지은이 장승진
펴낸이·장승진
펴낸곳·(주)프랙티쿠스
주소·서울시 서초구 잠원동 15-10 라성빌딩 4층
전화·02)6203-7774 | 팩스·02)6008-7779
홈페이지·www.practicus.co.kr | 이메일·help@practicus.co.kr
출판신고·2010년 7월 21일 제 2010-47호

ⓒ 장승진

저자와 출판사의 허락 없이는 이 책의 전부 또는 일부 내용을 어떠한 형태나 수단으로도 이용하지 못합니다.

ISBN 978-89-6893-044-7 13740

정가 16,700원

같은 생각
다른 표현

스몰토크 편

프랙티쿠스

머리말

스몰토크(small talk)라는 말이 이제 우리에게도 낯설지 않습니다. 사전적인 의미는 '어떤 사람과 친해지는 과정에서 나누는 가벼운 대화' 정도 되죠. 보통 날씨 얘기가 가장 대표적인 스몰토크 주제입니다. 하지만 이 책에서는 스몰토크의 범위를 그렇게 좁히지 않고, 일상에서 나눌 수 있는 너무 진지하지 않은 대화들이라고 생각해 보았습니다.

이 책은 우리의 일상을 말하는 기본적인 스몰토크 문장과, 취미, 대중문화, 그리고 연예인 등 다양한 주제에 관한 예문을 다룹니다. 실용적인 영어 능력이 필요한 많은 분들에게서 제가 들은 얘기는, "일과 관련된 영어는 어떻게든 하겠는데, 식사자리나 캐주얼한 자리에서 영어로 대화하기가 오히려 더 힘들다"였습니다. 그런 어려움을 느끼는 분들께 많은 도움이 되리라 생각합니다.

『같은 생각 다른 표현』이라는 시리즈 제목에서 보듯, 이 책은 '패러프레이징'을 통해 다양한 표현을 익히는 것을 목표로 합니다. 많은 분들이 자신의 영어 표현력이 제한되어 있고, 항상 하는 말만 하고 있다는 사실에 답답해합니다. 그런 답답함을 극복하는 가장 좋은 방법은 우리말 하나에 대응하는 다양한 영어 표현을 익히고 활용하는 것입니다. 『같은 생각 다른 표현』 시리즈는 바로 그런 목적을 위해 만들어졌습니다. 앞으로도 패러프레이징이라는 학습법을 활용한 다양한 시리즈 도서를 출간할 예정이니 많은 관심 부탁드립니다.

이 책을 통해 영어 대화의 소재들을 더욱 풍성하게 만드는 동시에 표현력도 신장시켜 보시기 바랍니다.

장승진

차례

일상을 말하는 스몰토크 — 11

사는 곳	12
직장	18
일	26
날씨	32
인사말	40
가족	46
연애	50
건강	60
용모	68
Exercise1	74

좋은 것을 말하는 스몰토크 — 79

취미	80
운동	86
맛집, 음식	92
여행	104
쇼핑	112
반려동물	120
Exercise2	128

대중문화와 스포츠를 말하는
스몰토크
133

스포츠	**134**
드라마	140
음악	146
영화	152
Exercise3	**162**

세상을 말하는
스몰토크
167

SNS	**168**
뉴스	172
연예인	176
K-Drama	**186**
K-Pop	**192**
Exercise4	**198**

이 책의 구성

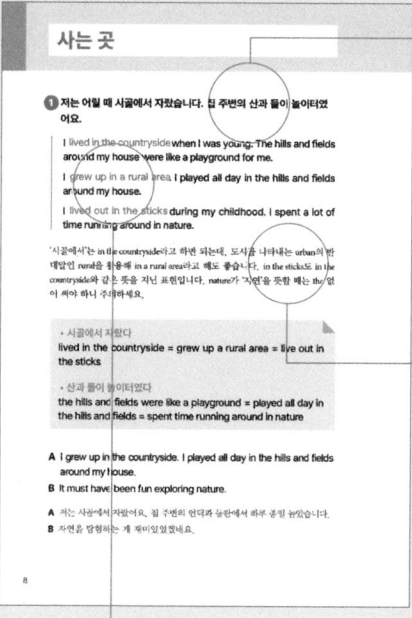

우리말 문장
스몰토크 상황에서 등장하는 문장을, 우선 우리말로 보여줍니다. 외국인과의 대화에 쓸 만하고, 그래서 영어로 표현해 볼 가치가 있는 문장들을 선정했습니다.

설명
영어 문장에 등장한 단어나 표현을 설명하는 부분입니다. 쉽고 정확한 이해를 돕고자 노력했습니다.

영어 대안
우리말을 영어로 표현한 세 가지 버전을 제시합니다. 우리말 '단어'를 영어 '단어'로 옮기는 게 중요한 게 아니라, 우리말의 '의미'를 자연스러운 영어 '문장'으로 표현하는 것이 중요합니다. 우리말 하나에 대응하는 영어 표현은 다양하게 존재하니, 여러 표현을 함께 익혀 두는 것이 영어가 유창해지는 비결입니다.

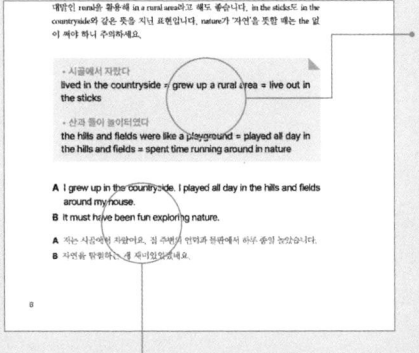

암기 박스

세 개의 영어 버전에서 핵심 표현만을 떼어 박스 안에 정리했습니다. 복습을 위해 책을 펼쳤을 때 핵심만 빨리 익힐 수 있도록 도움을 줄 것입니다.

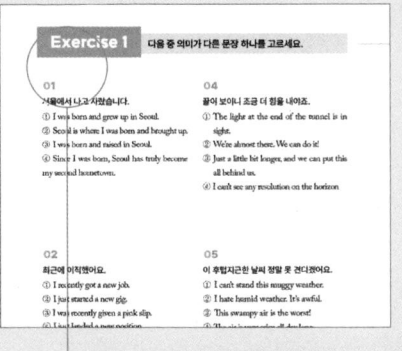

대화

앞서 소개한 문장을 실제 대화 속에서 익힐 수 있게, 자연스러운 대화문을 제시합니다. 세 가지 버전 중 하나만 활용해서 대화를 꾸몄고, 다른 버전들의 응용은 독자의 몫으로 남깁니다.

연습문제

중간중간 복습을 위해 풀어볼 수 있는 연습문제를 넣었습니다. 의미가 다른 영어 문장 한 개를 고르는 식으로 되어 있습니다. 앞서 제시한 영어 문장들을 다시 복습하고 기억하는 계기로 활용하기 바랍니다.

일상을 말하는 스몰토크

사는 곳
직장
일
날씨
인사말
가족
연애
건강
용모
Exercise 1

사는 곳

1 저는 어릴 때 시골에서 자랐습니다. 집 주변의 산과 들이 놀이터 같았어요.

> I lived in the countryside when I was young. The hills and fields around my house were like a playground for me.
>
> I grew up in a rural area. I played all day in the hills and fields around my house.
>
> I lived out in the sticks during my childhood. I spent a lot of time running around in nature.

'시골에서'는 in the countryside라고 하면 되는데, 도시를 나타내는 urban의 반대말인 rural을 활용해 in a rural area라고 해도 좋습니다. in the sticks도 in the countryside와 같은 뜻입니다. nature가 '자연'을 뜻할 때는 the 없이 써야 하니 주의하세요.

- **시골에서 자랐다**
  lived in the countryside = grew up a rural area = live out in the sticks

- **산과 들이 놀이터였다**
  the hills and fields were like a playground = played all day in the hills and fields = spent time running around in nature

A I grew up in the countryside. I played all day in the hills and fields around my house.
B It must have been fun exploring nature.

A 저는 시골에서 자랐어요. 집 주변의 언덕과 들판에서 하루 종일 놀았습니다.
B 자연을 탐험하는 게 재미있었겠네요.

② 저는 서울에서 나고 자랐는데, 전원에서 살아보고 싶습니다.

> I was born and grew up in Seoul. I would like to live in the countryside.
>
> I was born and bred in Seoul. I would like to live in a quieter area.
>
> I was born and raised in Seoul. I really want to live out in a more rural area.

'나고 자랐다'고 할 때는 was born and raised가 기본 표현입니다. 여기서 raised는 '양육되다' 정도 의미죠. raised 자리에 성장했다는 뜻의 grew up, 사육된다는 뜻인 bred를 활용해도 좋습니다.

- **서울에서 나고 자랐다**
was born and grew up in Seoul = was born and bred in Seoul
= was born and raised in Seoul

- **전원에서 살다**
live in the countryside = live in a quieter area = live out in a more rural area

---

A I was born and raised in Seoul. I really want to live out in a more rural area. I love the idea of having a closer connection to nature.

B Yeah, I agree. The city can be overwhelming sometimes.

A 서울에서 나고 자랐는데, 저는 정말 전원에서 살아보고 싶어요. 자연과 더 가까워진다는 점이 마음에 듭니다.

B 맞아요. 저도 그렇게 생각해요. 도시는 때로 부담이 되죠.

사는 곳

❸ 은퇴하면 전원 생활을 해 보고 싶습니다.

> I dream of living in the countryside when I retire.
> I dream of retiring to the countryside.
> My dream is to retire to a rural area.

은퇴하고 전원에서 사는 것을 동사 두 개로 표현하지 않고, retire to the countryside처럼 말할 수도 있습니다. 은퇴하고 전원으로 간다는 의미를 표현하는 전치사 to에 주의해야 합니다.

> • 은퇴하고 전원 생활을 하다
> live in the countryside when I retire = retire to the countryside = retire to a rural area

A Do you have any plans for your future retirement?
B I dream of retiring to the countryside.
A It sounds like a wonderful dream.
B Yeah, I really long for that peaceful lifestyle.

A 은퇴 후 계획 있으세요?
B 은퇴하면 전원에서 사는 걸 꿈꾸고 있어요.
A 정말 멋진 꿈인데요.
B 네, 정말 평화로운 삶을 살아보고 싶습니다.

4 출근하려면 지하철로 한 시간 정도 걸려요.

My house is about one hour away from my office by subway.

I can get to my office in an hour by subway train.

If I take the subway, it takes me about an hour to reach my office.

우리말에서 '출근'과 '퇴근'을 대신하는 표현은 거의 없죠. 하지만 영어에서는 일을 하러 가거나 사무실에서 떠난다는 의미를 전달하는 다양한 표현들이 출퇴근을 나타내는 말로 쓰입니다. 여기서도 '사무실에 도착한다'로 '출근'을 표현하고 있죠. get to와 reach를 활용하고 있습니다.

> • 지하철로 한 시간 걸린다
> one hour away by subway = in an hour by subway train = if I take the subway it takes me about an hour

A How long does it take for you to get to work every day?
B My house is about one hour away from my office by subway.
A That's not too bad.

A 출근하는 데 얼마나 걸리나요?
B 지하철로 집에서 사무실까지 약 1시간 거리입니다.
A 그렇게 나쁘진 않네요.

사는 곳

5 주거비 때문에 서울에서 멀리 떨어져 살고 싶은데, 출퇴근이 오래 걸려 못하겠어요.

> I would like to live far from Seoul because of the housing price, but I can't do it. I can't stand a long commute.
>
> I would rather live far away from Seoul because of the cost of housing, but I can't do it. I hate commuting long hours.
>
> I would like to move far away from Seoul because of the overpriced housing, but I can't. I can't stand commuting too far.

'주거'를 영어로 표현할 때 생각할 단어는 housing입니다. housing price, cost of housing처럼 비용과 관련된 단어를 붙여 말하면 '주거비'가 되죠. commute는 동사, 명사로 모두 쓰이므로, long commute가 '장거리 출퇴근'을 가리키고, commute long hours라고 하면 '장거리 출퇴근을 하다'라는 뜻입니다.

> • (비싼) 주거비
> housing price = cost of housing = overpriced housing
>
> • 출퇴근 시간이 길다
> a long commute = commute long hours = commute too far

A Have you ever thought about living outside of Seoul?
B Yes. I would rather live away from Seoul because of the cost of housing, but I can't do it. I hate commuting long hours.
A That's understandable. Commuting can be so tiring.

A 서울 밖으로 나가서 사는 것 생각해 본 적 있으세요?
B 예. 주거비 때문에 서울을 떠나 살고 싶은데 그럴 수가 없네요. 출퇴근 긴 걸 싫어하거든요.
A 이해가 가요. 출퇴근이 길면 피곤할 수 있죠.

6 공기 좋은 곳에 사는 것도 좋지만, 저는 출퇴근 짧은 게 더 중요해요.

It's good to live in a place where I can breathe clean air, but for me, a short commute is much more important.

It's better to live somewhere I can breathe clean air, but for me, it's much more important to have a short commute.

It'd be good if I could live in a place with fresh air, but right now, a shorter commuting distance is more important.

여기서도 commute를 명사와 동사로 모두 활용했습니다. '신선한 공기'는 clean air, fresh air로 표현할 수 있죠.

- **공기 좋은 곳에 살다**
live in a place where I can breathe clean air = live somewhere I can breathe clean air = live in a place with fresh air

- **출퇴근 시간이 짧다**
a short commute = have a short commute = a shorter commuting distance

A Have you ever considered moving out of Seoul?
B It's good to live in a place where I can breathe clean air, but for me, a short commute is much more important now.

A 서울 밖으로 이사하는 것 고려해 본 적이 있나요?
B 깨끗한 공기를 마실 수 있는 곳에서 살면 좋겠지만, 지금 저에게는 출퇴근 시간 짧은 게 더 중요합니다.

직장

7 최근에 이직했어요.

> I recently got a new job.
> I started a new job recently.
> I just started a new gig.

새로운 일을 시작하는 것이 '이직'이므로 get a new job, start a new job처럼 표현할 수 있습니다. job 대신 gig이라는 구어 표현도 자주 등장합니다. gig은 원래 '공연'을 말하는데, 예술가가 새로운 공연을 하는 것은 곧 새로운 일자리를 얻는 것이므로, '일', '일자리'라는 뜻으로 쓰입니다.

- **이직했다**
  got a new job = started a new job = started a new gig

A I recently got a new job.
B Congratulations! How do you like it so far?
A It's been great. The work is a bit challenging but very rewarding.

A 새 직장으로 옮겼어요.
B 축하해요! 지금까지 일하기는 어때요?
A 좋아요. 일은 약간 어렵지만 보람이 큽니다.

8 대학 졸업하고 계속 이 직장에 다니고 있습니다.

I've been working for this company since I joined right after graduation.

I've been working for this company since I graduated.

I've been with this company my entire career. I started here straight out of university.

어떤 회사에서 일하는 것은 work for the company, be with the company처럼 표현할 수 있습니다. 전치사 for와 with를 눈여겨보면 되죠. '졸업하자마자'라는 의미로 right after graduation이라고 했는데, '대학을 나오고 바로'라는 의미로 straight out of university/college라고 해도 좋습니다.

> • 졸업하고
> right after graduation = since I graduated = straight out of university

A How long have you been working at your current job?
B I've been with this company my entire career. I started here straight out of university.
A Wow. You must really enjoy working there.

A 지금 직장에서 얼마나 오래 일하셨나요?
B 내내 이 직장에만 있었어요. 대학 졸업하고 바로 여기서 일하기 시작했어요.
A 와. 일이 진짜 만족스러우신가 봐요.

직장

9 연봉을 더 받을 수 있는 곳이 있으면 옮길 생각입니다.

If I get an offer with a higher salary, I'm going to leave my current company.

If I could find better money elsewhere, I wouldn't hesitate to quit.

I'm holding out for a higher salary. If I get that, I'm gone.

'이직 제안'을 offer라고 하는데, 회사를 옮긴다고 할 때 잘 등장하는 단어입니다. higher salary, 좀 더 구어적으로 better money 모두 '더 많은 연봉'을 일컫죠. 회사를 그만두는 것도 다양하게 표현할 수 있는데, 중단한다는 뜻으로 quit이라고만 해도 의미가 충분히 전달됩니다. 세번째 문장의 hold out for는 기대한다는 뜻입니다.

- 연봉을 더 받을 곳이 있다
get an offer with higher salary = find better money elsewhere
= get a higher salary

- 이직하다
leave my current company = quit = be gone

A Have you been thinking about changing jobs?
B Yes. If I get an offer with higher salary, I'm going to quit.

A 이직을 생각하고 계신가요?
B 예. 더 높은 연봉을 제시하는 제안을 받는다면, 그만둘 거예요.

🔟 연봉도 중요하지만 워라밸이 보장되는 직장을 원했어요.

> A high salary is good, but I wanted a company where I can have a good work-life balance.
>
> A high salary does matter, but I wanted to work somewhere that offered a good work-life balance.
>
> A high salary sounds nice, but I knew I'd rather work at a company with a good work-life balance.

워라밸은 work-life balance라고 하면 됩니다. 그냥 워라밸이 아니라 좋은 워라밸이어야 의미가 있으므로, 앞에 good을 붙여 표현하는 경우가 많습니다.

> • 워라밸이 보장되다
> have a good work-life balance = work somewhere that offers a good work-life balance = work at a company with a good work-life balance

A A high salary is important, but I preferred a company that offered a good work-life balance.
B That makes a lot of sense. Work-life balance can really impact your happiness.

A 높은 연봉도 중요하지만, 저는 워라밸을 중시하는 회사를 더 선호했습니다.
B 충분히 이해가 가요. 일과 삶의 균형이 행복에 영향을 미칠 수 있죠.

직장

11 우리 회사는 직장 문화가 자유로운 편입니다.

> The office culture of my company is very free.
>
> The office culture at my company is extremely flexible.
>
> My company's office culture offers a substantial amount of freedom.

자유롭다고 할 때는 free, freedom을 활용할 수 있지만, 경직되지 않고 유연하다는 의미에서 flexible도 적절합니다. 세번째 문장의 substantial amount는 양이 꽤 되고 많다는 뜻입니다.

> • (문화가) 자유롭다
> be free = be flexible = offer a substantial amount of freedom

A How do you like your job?
B The office culture is extremely flexible. It has a positive impact on my work-life balance.
A That's great. Flexibility is so important nowadays.

A 하는 일은 어떠세요?
B 저희 회사는 사내 문화가 매우 유연해요. 일과 삶의 균형에 긍정적인 영향을 미칩니다.
A 좋네요. 요즘에는 유연성이 매우 중요하죠.

12 우리 회사는 여성 차별이 없는 편이에요. 여성 임원도 많습니다.

> Our company doesn't have much of glass ceiling issues. We have many female executives.
>
> Glass ceiling issues are rare in our company. We have a significant number of female executives.
>
> Our company stands out with its high number of female executives and minimal glass ceiling problems.

여성이 임원으로 승진하지 못하는 차별을 glass ceiling이라고 하죠. 그런 차별이 드물거나 거의 없으므로 rare, minimal과 같은 단어를 활용했습니다. 세번째 문장의 stand out은 두드러지거나 특출난 모습을 일컫죠. '우리 회사의 뛰어난 점'을 말하기 위해 썼습니다.

> • 여성 차별이 없는 편이다
> not have much of glass ceiling issue = glass ceiling issues are rare = minimal glass ceiling problems

A Glass ceiling issues are rare in our company. We have a significant number of female executives.
B It's great to see companies promoting gender equality. I hope more companies follow your company's example.

A 우리 회사는 유리 천장 문제가 거의 없어요. 여성 임원도 상당히 많고요.
B 양성 평등을 중시하는 기업이 있는 건 좋은 일입니다. 더 많은 회사들이 귀사의 사례를 따르면 좋겠네요.

직장

13 지금 하는 일이 꿈꾸던 직업은 아니지만 만족스러운 편입니다.

> My current job is not necessarily what I was dreaming of, but I'm pretty content with it.
>
> While my current job isn't exactly what I dreamed of, I'm quite satisfied with it.
>
> I'm not working in my dream position, but I'm still quite pleased with my job.

꿈꾸던 것을 말할 때 dream을 앞에 붙여 간략히 표현할 수 있죠. dream car, dream girl, dream job 등 다양하게 활용됩니다. 세번째 문장의 dream position은 '꿈꾸던 자리' 정도 의미입니다. 만족스럽다고 할 때 satisfied말고 content도 자주 쓰입니다. be content with 형태로 활용하면 되죠.

- **꿈꾸던 직업은 아니다**
  not necessarily what I was dreaming of = not exactly what I dreamed of = not working in my dream position

- **만족스럽다**
  content with = satisfied with = pleased with

A How do you feel about your job?
B While my current job isn't exactly what I dreamed of, I'm quite satisfied with it.
A That's good to hear. Sometimes, finding contentment where you are is all that matters.

A 지금 직업에 대해 어떻게 생각하세요?
B 정확히 제가 꿈꾸던 직업인 건 아니지만 상당히 만족합니다.
A 좋네요. 때로는 자신이 있는 곳에서 만족을 찾는 것이 가장 중요하죠.

14 어릴 때부터 꿈꾸던 일을 하고 있어요. 이 분야로 진출하기 위해 많은 노력을 했습니다.

> My job is what I wanted to have since I was a child. I made a lot of efforts to get into this field.
>
> Ever since I was a child, I aspired to have this job. I put in a lot of effort to enter this field.
>
> This job has been my dream since childhood, and I've worked hard to achieve it.

두번째 문장의 aspire는 무언가를 열망한다는 뜻입니다. dream과 같은 의미로 활용하고 있죠. 어떤 분야에 발을 들인다고 할 때는 get into this field, enter this field와 같이 표현할 수 있습니다.

- **어릴 때부터 꿈꾸던 일**
what I wanted to have since I was a child = aspired to have this job = has been my dream since childhood

- **이 분야로 진출하다**
get into this field = enter this field = achieve it

A How did you end up in your current job?
B Ever since I was a child, I aspired to have this job, and I put in a lot of effort to enter this field.
A Great. You achieved your childhood dreams!

A 어떻게 이 일을 하시게 되었나요?
B 저는 어렸을 때부터 이 직업을 갖고 싶었고, 이 분야에 발을 들이기 위해 많은 노력을 기울였습니다.
A 대단합니다. 어린 시절 꿈을 이뤘군요!

일

⑮ 하는 일이 잘 안 되고 있어요.

> Nothing's going my way.
> Nothing's working out for me.
> Things aren't going very well.

잘 되어 가는 것은 말 그대로 go well이라고 할 수 있죠. go one's way도 같은 의미인데, 내가 원하는 방향으로 가는 것이 곧 일이 잘 되는 것이기 때문입니다. work out은 다양한 뜻을 지니는데, 일이 잘 된다는 의미도 있습니다.

> • 일이 잘 안 되다
> not going my way = not working out for me = not going very well

A How have you been lately?
B Seems like nothing's going my way. It's been really tough.
A I'm sorry to hear that. I'm hoping things will get better soon.

A 요즘 어떻게 지내세요?
B 뜻대로 되는 게 아무것도 없는 것 같아요. 정말 힘들었습니다.
A 안타깝네요. 상황이 곧 나아지길 바라겠습니다.

16 오늘 일 정말 많았어요.

It was a long day.
I was swamped today.
I was buried under a pile of work today.

첫번째 대안처럼 '긴 하루였다'라고만 하면 일 많고 힘든 하루였다는 뜻이 됩니다. swamp는 원래 늪을 가리키는데, 늪에 빠져 허우적대는 모습과 일이 많아 힘들어하는 모습을 연관지어 표현한 겁니다. 세번째 문장에서는 '일더미에 깔렸다'라고 했죠.

> • 일이 많았다
> a long day = be swamped = be buried under a pile of work

A How was your day?
B It was a long day. I'm exhausted.
A What made it so long?
B Work was really hectic, and I had to fill in my co-worker who was out of office today.

A 오늘 하루 어땠어요?
B 긴 하루였습니다. 피곤하네요.
A 무슨 일 때문에 그랬나요?
B 일이 정말 바빴고, 오늘 휴가 낸 동료 자리까지 채워야 했어요.

일

17 중요한 프로젝트 때문에 바빴다가 이제서야 한숨 돌리네요.

I've been terribly busy due to an important project, and now I have time to relax.

I've been super busy because of this important project, but I've got time to relax now.

I've been stuck at work due to a major project, but I'm free to relax now.

바쁜 상황을 강조할 때 붙이는 단어에 두번째 문장의 super도 있습니다. 매우 어떠하다는 의미로 very 대신 활용해 보기 바랍니다. 안정이나 휴식을 취한다고 할 때 가장 일반적인 동사는 relax입니다.

- **매우 바쁘다**
terribly busy = super busy = be stuck at work

- **숨 돌릴 시간이 있다**
have time to relax = get time to relax = be free to relax

A I've been so busy recently because of this project. Now I finally have time to relax.
B I'm glad you have some time to unwind now. Do you have any plans for your free time?

A 큰 프로젝트 때문에 최근에 너무 바빴어요. 이제야 쉴 시간이 생겼습니다.
B 쉴 수 있는 시간이 생겼다니 기쁩니다. 휴식하며 뭐 할지 계획 있으세요?

18 끝이 보이니 조금 더 힘을 내야죠.

> The light at the end of the tunnel is in sight. Let's power through.
>
> We're almost there. We can do it!
>
> Just a little bit longer, and we can put this all behind us.

'터널 끝의 빛'을 가리키는 light at the end of the tunnel은 어려운 상황이 끝나 감을 일컫는 비유 표현입니다. in sight는 시야에 들어온다는 뜻이죠. power through는 힘을 내고 해 나간다는 뜻의 구동사입니다. 세번째 문장의 put this behind us는 '어떤 일을 뒤에 놓다', 즉 모두 끝내고 지난 일로 만든다는 의미입니다.

> • 끝이 보인다
> light at the end of the tunnel is in sight = almost there = can put this behind us
>
> • 힘을 내자
> power through = we can do it = just a little bit longer

A How's the project going?
B The light at the end of the tunnel is in sight. We're almost done.
A That's great to hear.
B Yes, just a little more effort, and we can put this all behind us.

A 프로젝트는 어떻게 진행되고 있나요?
B 터널 끝의 빛이 보입니다. 거의 끝났어요.
A 반가운 소식이네요.
B 예, 조금만 더 노력하면 끝낼 수 있어요.

일

일은 힘들지만 배우는 게 많아 만족합니다.

> Work is hard, but I learn a lot in this company. I'm satisfied.
>
> Work is tough, but I'm learning something new here, so it's worth it.
>
> The workload is heavy, but I'm gaining experience. That evens it out to me.

세번째 문장의 workload는 일의 양이나 부담을 가리킵니다. 일이 많다고 할 때 heavy와 함께 잘 활용됩니다. 이어 나온 표현 even out은 평평하게 만들거나 평균을 낸다는 뜻이죠. 일이 힘든 것과 경험을 얻는 것을 상쇄하면 결국 평평해진다, 즉 손해보는 게 아니라는 뜻으로 한 말입니다.

> • 일이 힘들다
> work is hard = work is tough = the workload is heavy
>
> • 배우는 게 많다
> learn a lot = learn something new = gain experience

A Work is tough, but I'm learning a lot here, so it's worth it.
B Absolutely. Challenges help us grow.

A 일은 힘들지만 이 회사에서 배우는 게 많아 그만한 가치가 있습니다.
B 그럼요. 어려움을 겪으면서 성장하는 거니까요.

20 회사에서 어려운 문제를 해결하고 나면 보람을 느낍니다.

When I complete a difficult project at work, I feel a strong sense of reward and accomplishment.

I love the feeling of achievement after finishing something challenging at work.

Completing a tough task at work gives me a rewarding sense of accomplishment.

성취감을 sense of achievement/accomplishment와 같이 표현할 수 있죠. 이와 유사하게 '보람'을 말할 때 잘 등장하는 단어가 reward입니다. 명사, 동사로 모두 쓰이므로 sense of reward 혹은 rewarding sense라고 표현할 수 있죠.

- **(일을 마치고 느끼는) 보람**
a sense of reward and accomplishment = the feeling of achievement = a rewarding sense of accomplishment

- **어려운 문제를 해결하다**
complete a difficult project at work = finish something challenging at work = complete a tough task at work

A How's work going for you lately?
B I have some challenges, but I love the feeling of achievement after finishing something challenging at work.
A Me too. The sense of achievement makes hard work worthwhile.

A 요즘 일은 어때요?
B 몇 가지 어려움이 있지만, 힘든 일을 끝낸 후 성취감을 느끼는 게 좋아요.
A 저도요. 성취감 덕에 열심히 일하게 되죠.

날씨

21 일기예보에서 비가 올 거라던데. 정말 그래 보여요.

> I heard that rain is in the forecast. It really looks so.
>
> I heard it's going to rain. It certainly seems like it.
>
> I heard they're predicting rain. It sure appears that way.

첫번째 문장의 in the forecast는 일기예보에서 본 내용을 말할 때 등장합니다. '비/눈이 올 거라고 한다'를 Rain/Snow is in the forecast.와 같이 표현할 수 있죠. 세번째 문장의 appears that way는 '그렇게 보인다'는 뜻입니다.

> • 비가 온다는 예보가 있다
> rain is in the forecast = it's going to rain = they're predicting rain
>
> • 그럴 것 같다
> it looks so = it seems like it = it appears that way

A I heard that rain is in the forecast. It really looks so.
B Yeah, the sky is definitely looking gloomy today.
A I guess I'll have to bring my umbrella just in case.

A 비가 온다는 예보가 있는데. 정말 그럴 것 같아요.
B 네, 오늘은 하늘이 확실히 꾸물꾸물해요.
A 혹시 모르니 우산을 챙겨야겠어요.

22 고향 날씨는 어때요?

How's the weather back in your hometown?

How's the weather where you're from?

What sort of weather do you usually see at home?

고향은 hometown이라고 해도 좋고, where you're from이라고 할 수도 있죠. 세번째 문장의 at home도 문맥에 따라 '집에서'가 아니라 '고향에서'를 뜻하게 됩니다.

> • 고향에서는
> back in your hometown = where you're from = at home

A How's the weather back in your hometown?
B Oh, it's pretty chilly right now. Winter's in full swing. I miss the snowy winters.

A 고향 날씨는 어때요?
B 지금은 꽤 추워요. 겨울이 한창이죠. 눈 내리는 겨울이 그립네요.

날씨

23 이 더위가 사라지기는 할까요?

Do you think this heat wave will ever end?

Will this heat ever break?

When will we get some relief from this heat?

더위가 지속되는 상황을 가리키는 단어가 heat wave이죠. 두번째 문장의 break는 잦아들거나 끝이 난다는 의미입니다. 날씨에 변화가 있거나 몸의 열이 떨어지는 것을 나타내는 동사로 쓰입니다.

> **• 더위가 끝날 거다**
> heat wave will end = heat will break = get some relief from this heat

A Do you think this heatwave will ever end?
B I sure hope so. It's been unbearable lately.
A Yeah. I've been staying inside as much as possible.
B Same here. I miss being able to go for a walk without feeling like I'm melting.

A 이 더위가 끝나기는 할까요?
B 그러기를 바라죠. 요즘 날씨는 정말 참기 힘들어요.
A 네. 가능한 한 실내에만 있었어요.
B 저도 그래요. 녹아 내리는 것 같은 기분 없이 산책할 수 있던 때가 그립네요.

24 이 후텁지근한 날씨 정말 못 견디겠어요.

I can't stand this muggy weather. It's terrible.

I hate humid weather. It's awful.

This swampy air is the worst!

습도가 높고 더운 날씨를 나타내는 대표 단어가 muggy입니다. humid는 습도가 높다는 뜻이고, swampy는 습지를 뜻하는 swamp에서 나온 단어로, 습도가 높고 끈끈하다는 의미입니다.

> • 후텁지근한 날씨
> muggy weather = humid weather = swampy air

A I can't stand this muggy weather. It's terrible.
B I know. It feels like I'm in hot sauna.
A Yeah. It's hard to get anything done when it's this uncomfortable.

A 이 습한 날씨 못 참겠어요. 정말 너무하네요.
B 맞아요. 뜨거운 사우나에 있는 것 같죠.
A 네. 이렇게 불편하면 어떤 일도 하기 힘들어요.

날씨

25 춥고 건조한 날씨 못 견디겠어요. 빨리 봄이 왔으면 좋겠어요.

I can't stand the cold and dry weather anymore. I wish spring was here.

I can't tolerate this cold, dry weather any longer. I wish it were spring already.

I'm fed up with the cold and dry weather. I wish spring would come soon.

'봄이 왔으면 좋겠다'처럼 소망하는 내용을 말할 때는 I wish로 문장을 시작하고 소망하는 내용은 Spring was here.처럼 과거형으로 표현하는 것이 원칙입니다. 세번째 문장에서 would를 쓴 것도 같은 이유죠. be 동사인 경우 were, was모두 가능합니다. 세번째 문장의 be fed up with는 너무 오래 혹은 많이 겪어서 질렸다는 의미입니다.

> • 못 견디겠다
> can't stand = can't tolerate = be fed up with
>
> • 봄이 왔으면 좋겠다
> I wish spring was here = I wish it were spring already = I wish spring would come soon

A I can't stand the cold and dry weather anymore. I wish spring was here.
B Me too. I miss the warmth and the blooming flowers.
A Exactly. Everything feels so dull and lifeless right now.

A 춥고 건조한 날씨 더 이상 못 참겠어요. 봄이 왔으면 좋겠어요.
B 저도 그래요. 봄의 따뜻함과 피어나는 꽃들이 그리워요.
A 맞아요. 지금은 모든 게 너무 칙칙하고 생기가 없어요.

26 요즘이 덥지도 춥지도 않고 야외 활동하기 딱 좋은 것 같습니다.

> These are the best times for outdoor activities. It's not too warm and not too cold.
>
> Right now is the perfect time for outdoor activities. The weather is just right—not too hot, not too cold.
>
> This is the ideal weather for enjoying outdoor activities, with temperatures being perfectly moderate.

이상적인 것은 ideal로 표현할 수 있습니다. 지나치게 덥거나 춥지 않은 날씨를 세번째 문장에서는 moderate으로 표현하고 있죠. 극단적이지 않고 온화하거나 온건한 상태를 묘사하는 단어입니다.

• 딱 좋은 시기
these are the best times for = right now is the perfect time for = this is the ideal weather for

• 덥지도 춥지도 않다
not too warm and not too cold = not too hot, not too cold = temperatures are perfectly moderate

---

A These are the best times for outdoor activities. It's not too warm and not too cold.
B Absolutely. The weather is perfect for hiking and picnics.

A 요즘이 야외 활동 하기에 가장 좋은 시기예요. 너무 덥지도 춥지도 않아요.
B 맞아요. 하이킹과 피크닉에 완벽한 날씨죠.

날씨

27 아직 가을이라고 생각했는데, 날씨가 갑자기 추워졌네요.

> I thought we're still in fall, but the weather has gotten so cold suddenly.
>
> I thought it was still fall, but the temperature dropped suddenly.
>
> I believed it was still autumn, but the sudden chill has taken me by surprise.

세번째 문장의 chill은 쌀쌀한 날씨나 서늘함을 가리킵니다. take someone by surprise가 급습한다는 뜻이므로, '찬 기운이 급습했다'라고 표현한 셈입니다.

> **• 날씨가 갑자기 추워지다**
> the weather has gotten cold suddenly = the temperature dropped suddenly = the sudden chill has taken me by surprise

A I thought it was still fall, but the weather has suddenly turned cold.
B I know. It's like winter just showed up overnight.
A Seriously, I wasn't prepared for this at all. I haven't even taken out my winter clothes yet!

A 아직 가을인 줄 알았는데 날씨가 갑자기 추워졌어요.
B 그러게요. 하룻밤 사이에 겨울이 온 것 같아요.
A 전 준비가 전혀 안 됐어요. 아직 겨울 옷도 꺼내지 않았어요!

28 더운 것과 추운 것 중 어떤 게 더 나으세요?

Do you prefer hot or cold weather?

Would you rather enjoy hot weather or cold weather?

Which do you favor, summer temperatures or winter chills?

favor와 prefer 는 어떤 것을 더 선호하는지 말할 때 유용한 동사들이죠. would rather는 차라리 ~하겠다는 뜻이므로, 두번째 문장은 둘 중 차라리 어떤 것을 즐기겠냐는 질문입니다.

> • 더위와 추위 중 어떤 것을 더 좋아하다
> prefer hot or cold weather = would rather enjoy hot weather or cold weather = favor, summer temperatures or winter chills

A Do you prefer hot or cold weather?
B I'd say cold weather. I love bundling up in cozy sweaters!
A Fair point, but I'd pick hot weather. Beaches and sunshine are unbeatable.

A 더운 날씨와 더운 날씨 중 어떤 게 더 나으세요?
B 추운 게 나아요. 따뜻한 스웨터를 입고 아늑하게 있는 것 좋아하거든요.
A 맞는 말씀이네요. 저는 더운 날씨를 선호합니다. 해변과 햇살보다 더 나은 건 없잖아요.

인사말

29 곧 다시 볼 수 있기를 바랍니다. 건강히 지내세요.

> I hope I can see you again soon. Stay healthy!
>
> I look forward to seeing you again soon. Stay well!
>
> I can't wait to see you again. Stay healthy!

기대한다고 할 때 가장 일반적으로 쓰는 표현이 두번째 문장의 look forward to이죠. 세번째 문장의 can't wait to는 '기대가 되어 기다리기가 힘들다'라는 뜻으로, 매우 기대가 된다는 의미입니다.

> **• 다시 만나기를 기대하다**
> hope to see you = look forward to seeing you = can't wait to see you

A It was so great catching up with you today.
B I had a wonderful time too. I hope I can see you again soon. Stay healthy!

A 오늘 오랜만에 만나서 정말 좋았어요.
B 저도 정말 즐거운 시간 보냈어요. 곧 다시 만날 수 있으면 좋겠습니다. 건강하세요!

30 오늘 생각지 않게 만나서 좋았어요. 곧 다시 봐요.

> It was great running into you today. Let's catch up again soon.
>
> It was great to see you again today. Let's set a coffee date.
>
> It was wonderful to run into you today! Let's chat again soon.

사람을 우연히 만나는 것을 run into라고 하죠. '따라잡다'라는 뜻을 지닌 catch up은 오랜만에 만나 어떻게 지냈는지 서로 얘기 나누는 것을 말하기도 합니다.

> • 우연히 다시 만나다
> running into you = see you again today

A It was great running into you today. Let's catch up again soon.
B Absolutely. It's been too long.
A How about we grab coffee next week?
B Sounds perfect.

A 생각지 않게 얼굴 봐서 좋았어요. 곧 다시 만나요.
B 물론이죠. 너무 오랜만이었죠.
A 다음 주에 커피 한 잔 할까요?
B 좋습니다.

인사말

31 힘드실 텐데 잘 지내시길 바랍니다.

> I hope you're holding up okay in this difficult time.
> I hope you're doing okay!
> I hope you're getting through this tough time.

힘든 시간을 잘 버티는 모습은 hold up okay라고 쉽게 표현할 수 있습니다. difficult time은 말 그대로 어려운 시기를 가리키는데, 가족이 사망한 상황, 즉 상중임을 말하는 표현이 되기도 합니다.

> • 힘들어도 잘 지내다
> hold up okay = do okay = get through this tough time

A I hope you're holding up okay in this difficult time.
B Thanks. It's been tough, but I'm managing.
A If you need anything, don't hesitate to reach out. I'm here for you.

A 어려운 시기에 잘 지내시길 바랍니다.
B 고마워요. 힘들었지만 잘 지내고 있어요.
A 도움이 필요하면 주저 말고 연락하세요. 제가 여기 있잖아요.

32 오랜만에 만나서 좋았어요. 좀 더 자주 봅시다.

> It was great seeing you for the first time in a while. Let's meet up more often.
>
> It's been great to finally catch up with you! Let's do this again soon.
>
> It was wonderful to finally see you! Let's set a date for next time.

'오랜만에'는 영어로 for the first time in a while이라고 할 수 있습니다. 이렇게 오랜만에 만나는 것을 두번째 문장에서는 간략히 catch up으로 표현하고 있죠.

> • 오랜만에 만나다
> see you for the first time in a while = catch up with you = finally see you

A It was great seeing you for the first time in a while. Let's meet up more often.
B Absolutely. I've missed hanging out with you.
A Same here. We should make it a regular thing.

A 오랜만에 만나서 반가웠어요. 더 자주 만납시다.
B 물론이죠. 같이 시간 보내고 싶었어요.
A 저도요. 우리 정기적으로 만나죠.

인사말

33 이메일이나 소셜미디어로 연락하고 지냅시다.

> Let's keep in touch via e-mail or social media.
>
> Drop me a line via email or social media.
>
> Look me up on social media, or just shoot me an email.

계속 연락하고 지내자고 할 때 쓰는 가장 일반적인 표현이 keep in touch입니다. 통신수단을 이용한다고 할 때 via를 활용해 via email, via social media, via Zoom처럼 말할 수 있죠. 세번째 문장에서는 shoot an email이라고 했는데, write 대신 shoot을 활용하기도 합니다. look up은 찾아본다는 뜻이죠.

> • (이메일이나 소셜미디어로) 연락하다
> keep in touch= drop me a line = look me up on social media

A It was nice catching up with you today.
B Same here. Let's keep in touch via e-mail or social media.
A Definitely! I'll send you a friend request and an email.

A 오늘 만나서 반가웠어요.
B 저도요. 이메일이나 소셜 미디어로 연락하고 지냅시다.
A 물론이죠! 친구 요청과 이메일을 보내드릴게요.

34 말씀 많이 들었어요. 실제로 뵙게 되니 반갑네요.

> I've heard a lot about you. It's nice to meet you in person.
>
> I've heard so much about you. It's a pleasure to finally meet you face-to-face.
>
> It's wonderful to meet you in person. I've heard plenty about you.

직접 만나는 것은 meet you in person이라고 할 수 있는데, 면대면으로 만난다는 의미에서 두번째 문장처럼 face-to-face라고 해도 좋습니다. 세번째 문장처럼 문장의 순서를 바꿔, 실제로 만나게 되니 좋다는 얘기를 먼저 해도 되죠.

- **얘기 많이 들었다**
  heard a lot about you = heard so much about you = heard plenty about you

- **실제로 만나다**
  meet you in person = meet you face-to-face

A Hi, I've heard a lot about you! It's nice to meet you in person.
B Oh, thank you! I hope it's all good things.
A Absolutely! People only had good things to say about you.

A 안녕하세요. 말씀 많이 들었어요. 실제로 뵙게 되니 반갑네요.
B 감사합니다. 좋은 얘기들만 들으셨길 바랍니다.
A 물론이죠! 다들 좋은 말씀만 하시던걸요.

가족

35 형제나 자매가 있으세요?

Do you have siblings?

Do you have brothers or sisters?

Are you an only child, or do you have siblings?

형제 자매를 siblings라고 표현하는 경우도 많습니다. 두번째 문장처럼 brothers and sisters라고 말하는 것보다 더 간결하고 캐주얼한 표현이죠.

> • 형제 자매가 있다
> have siblings = have brothers or sisters

A Do you have brothers or sisters?
B Yes, I have one older brother and a younger sister. How about you?
A I have two sisters. It's always interesting growing up with siblings.

A 형제 자매가 있나요?
B 네, 저는 오빠 한 명, 여동생 한 명 있습니다. 형제 자매 있으세요?
A 저는 자매가 둘 있습니다. 형제 자매와 함께 성장하는 것은 항상 즐겁죠.

36 저희 집은 딸만 셋입니다.

> Our family has only three daughters.
>
> We've got three kids, all girls.
>
> I have three daughters.

첫번째 문장은 부모나 자녀 모두 할 수 있는 말이고, 두번째와 세번째 문장은 부모의 입장에서 세 자녀가 모두 딸이라고 할 때 쓸 수 있는 문장이죠.

> • 딸만 셋이다
> have only three daughters = have got three kids, all girls

A Our family has only three daughters.
B That's wonderful. Sisters often share such a unique and deep connection.
A Yeah. We're very close and support each other.

A 우리 가족은 딸만 셋이에요.
B 좋네요. 자매끼리는 독특하고 깊은 유대감을 공유하는 경우가 많잖아요.
A 네. 서로 가깝게 지내면서 지지해 주죠.

가족

37 제가 늦게 결혼해서 아이가 아직 어려요.

> I married late, so my child is still very young.
>
> I married later in life, so my child is still quite young.
>
> My child is still very young because I married at an older age.

'늦게 결혼하다'는 marry late라고 간단히 표현할 수 있습니다. late 대신 at an older age라고 할 수도 있죠.

> • 늦게 결혼하다
> marry late = marry later in life = marry at an older age

A I married late, so the only child I have is still very young.
B How old is your child?
A He's three years old now and full of energy.
B He must be keeping you busy.

A 제가 늦게 결혼해서, 아이가 하나인데 아직 아주 어립니다.
B 몇 살이에요?
A 지금 세 살이고 에너지가 넘치죠.
B 바쁘시겠네요.

38 부모님을 되도록 자주 찾아 뵈려 하는데 잘 안 되네요.

> I try to visit my parents more often, but actually it's hard to be put into action.
>
> I aim to see my parents more frequently, but it's actually quite challenging to carry out.
>
> I try to spend more time with my parents, but in reality, it's tough to make it happen.

실천하는 것은 put something into action이라고 할 수 있습니다. 실행한다는 뜻의 carry out, 일이 일어나도록 한다는 의미인 make it happen도 같은 뜻이죠. 두번째 문장의 challenging은 difficult의 의미입니다. problem 대신 challenge, difficult 대신 challenging을 쓰는 경우가 많습니다.

- **부모님을 자주 찾아 뵙다**
  visit my parents more often = see my parents more frequently = spend more time with my parents

- **실천이 힘들다**
  hard to be put into action = challenging to carry out = tough to make it happen

A I try to visit my parents more often, but actually it's hard to be put into action.
B I get that. Life can get really busy sometimes.
A Exactly. I wish I could see them more often.

A 부모님을 더 자주 찾아 뵈려 노력하는데, 실천하기가 어렵습니다.
B 이해해요. 살면서 바쁠 때가 많잖아요.
A 맞아요. 좀 더 자주 뵈면 좋겠습니다.

연애

39 둘이 얼마나 사귀었나요?

How long have you two been together?

How long have you two been dating?

Have you guys been a couple for a while?

남녀가 사귀는 상황을 나타내는 표현도 다양하죠. be in a relationship이라고 할 수도 있지만, 함께한다는 의미로 be together처럼 쉽게 말할 수도 있습니다.

> • 남녀가 사귀다
> be together = be dating = be a couple

A How long have you two been together?
B We've been together for five years now.
A Wow. Any plans to celebrate the fifth anniversary?

A 두 분이 얼마나 사귀셨어요?
B 지금 5년째 만나고 있어요.
A 와. 5주년을 축하할 계획이 있으세요?

40 사귄 지 꽤 되었는데, 만나면 하는 일이 항상 비슷한 것 같아요. 좀 새로운 걸 찾아야 되겠습니다.

> We've been in a relationship for a while. Things I do with my girlfriend seem to be the same. We need to find some new activity for a change.
>
> We've been together for a while. These days we seem to be stuck doing the same old things, so we're looking for new activities to try out.
>
> We've been dating for a few years now. We're worried we're stuck in a rut, so we're trying to find something new to do together.

be stuck이나 be stuck in a rut은 모두 정해진 틀에 끼여(stuck) 발전이 없는 상황을 가리킵니다. 첫번째 대안의 for a change는 '변화를 주고자' 정도 의미죠.

> • 남녀가 사귀다
> be in a relationship = be together = be dating
>
> • 비슷한 것만 한다
> be the same = be stuck doing the same old things = be stuck in a rut

A Things I do with my girlfriend seem to be the same. That's why we're trying to find something new to do together.
B Sounds exciting. Have you thought about any new activities?

A 여자친구 만나서 항상 똑 같은 일만 하는 것 같아요. 그래서 함께 할 새로운 것을 찾으려 노력 중이에요.
B 좋네요. 새로운 것들을 생각해 보셨나요?

연애

41 예쁘고 몸매 좋은 여자를 좋아합니다.

I love women who are pretty and have a good body figure.

I like pretty women with an hourglass shape.

I like beautiful women with a shapely figure.

hourglass는 모래시계를 뜻하죠. 여성의 체형을 모래시계의 모양에 빗대어 표현하기도 합니다. shapely도 좋은 모양을 갖추었다는 뜻으로 여성의 몸매를 표현하는 단어입니다. 이런 표현들은 기억해 두되, 부적절하게 사용하지 않도록 주의해야 합니다.

> **• 여성의 몸매가 좋다**
> have a good body figure = with an hourglass shape = with a shapely figure

A How did the date go?
B It was okay.
A Are you going to ask her out again?
B You know, I simply like pretty women with an hourglass shape.

A 데이트는 어땠어요?
B 괜찮았어요.
A 또 데이트 신청할 건가요?
B 아시잖아요, 저는 그냥 예쁘고 몸매 좋은 여자 좋아하는거.

42 키 크고 잘생긴 남자를 좋아합니다.

> I love guys who are tall and good-looking.
>
> I prefer guys I can literally look up to, who are good-looking as well.
>
> Tall, dark, and handsome does it for me.

두번째 문장은 '말 그대로 올려다볼 수 있는 남자'라는 뜻으로, 결국 '키 큰 남자'를 말하고 있습니다. 세번째 문장의 tall, dark, and handsome은 외모가 출중한 남자를 가리키는 관용 표현입니다. 여기서 dark는 피부색이 검다는 뜻이 아니라, 머리카락 색깔이 짙다는 의미입니다. 뒤이어 나온 does it은 '충분하다', '적당하다'라는 뜻입니다.

> • 키 크고 잘생겼다
> tall and good-looking = who I can literally look up to and who is good-looking = tall, dark, and handsome

A I love tall, handsome men. There's just something about that combination that's so appealing.
B I get that. Height and good looks can definitely make a strong first impression.

A 저는 키 크고 잘생긴 남자 좋아해요. 둘 다 갖추면 특별한 매력이 있거든요.
B 이해 가요. 키와 외모가 확실히 강렬한 첫인상을 남기니까요.

연애

43 남자친구와 서로 말이 잘 통해서 좋습니다.

> I love my boyfriend because we can talk a lot of things together.
>
> I love my boyfriend because we're always on the same page.
>
> I love my boyfriend because we communicate so well.

두번째 문장의 on the same page는 같은 생각을 하고 있다는 뜻입니다. 같은 페이지를 펼치고 있어야 책의 내용을 서로 얘기할 수 있다는 데서 유래한 표현이죠.

> **• 말이 잘 통한다**
> can talk a lot of things together = be on the same page = communicate so well

A I love my boyfriend because we're always on the same page.
B That's great! It must be so comforting to be with someone who understands you so well.
A It really is. It makes spending time together so much fun.

A 항상 생각이 잘 통해서 남자친구를 사랑해요.
B 멋지네요! 자신을 잘 이해하는 사람과 함께 있으면 정말 편안할 거예요.
A 정말 그래요. 함께 시간을 보내는 게 정말 즐겁죠.

44 여자 친구와 공통의 관심사가 많아요.

My girlfriend and I have many things in common.

My girlfriend and I share so many interests.

My girlfriend and I have many mutual hobbies.

have many things in common이 공유하는 점이 많다는 의미인데, 결국 관심사(interests)가 같거나 공통의 취미(mutual hobbies)가 있다는 뜻도 됩니다.

> • 공통의 관심사가 많다
> have many things in common = share so many interests = have many mutual hobbies

A So, what's your secret to a happy relationship?
B My girlfriend and I have many things in common.
A That's great. It must be nice to share so many interests.
B It really is. We both love outdoor activities and even enjoy the same movies.

A 여자친구와 행복하게 지내는 비결이 뭐예요?
B 여자친구와 저는 공통점이 많아요.
A 좋네요. 여러 관심사를 공유하는 건 좋은 거죠.
B 정말 그래요. 둘 다 야외 활동을 좋아하고 같은 영화를 즐겨요.

연애

45 나이를 먹고 보니 여자친구의 외모보다는 성격이 중요한 것 같아요.

> As I grow older, now I realize that I have to look for a good personality in my girlfriend rather than great appearance.
>
> With age, I've come to understand that it's more important to seek a girlfriend with a good personality rather than to focus on looks.
>
> Over time, I realize the significance of valuing my girlfriend's character over her appearance.

외모를 appearance, looks와 같이 표현할 수 있습니다. -s를 붙여 looks라고 해야 한다는 점에 주의하세요.

- **나이를 먹고 보니**
as I grow older = with age = over time

- **외모보다는 성격이 중요하다**
look for good personality rather than great appearance =
seek a good personality rather than focus on looks = value character over one's appearance

---

A As I grow older, I realize that I have to look for a good personality in my girlfriend rather than great appearance.
B That's a wise realization. Looks can be deceiving, but a good personality lasts.

A 나이가 들면서, 여자 볼 때 외모보다 좋은 성격을 추구해야 한다는 걸 깨달았습니다.
B 현명하네요. 외모는 잠깐 속일 수 있지만, 좋은 성격은 오래 갑니다.

46 오래 사귄 남자 친구와 올해 결혼할 예정입니다.

I have a boyfriend that I have been steady with, and we're getting married this year.

I've been in a long-term relationship with my boyfriend, and we're getting married this year.

My boyfriend and I have been together for a long time, and we're tying the knot this year.

꾸준하다는 뜻인 steady는 이성 친구를 꾸준히 사귄다는 뜻도 지닙니다. 세번째 문장의 tie the knot은 직역하면 '매듭을 맺다'인데, '결혼하다'라는 뜻의 관용 표현이죠.

- 오래 사귄 남자친구가 있다
boyfriend that I have been steady with = in a long-term relationship with my boyfriend = have been together for a long time

- 결혼한다
we're getting married = we're tying the knot

A I have a boyfriend that I have been steady with, and we're getting married this year.
B Wow, that's amazing news! Congratulations!

A 오래 사귄 남자친구가 있는데, 올해 결혼할 거예요.
B 멋진 소식이네요! 축하해요!

연애

47 지난번에 남자 친구 사귈 때, 개인 생활이 없는 것 같았어요. 지금은 혼자인 게 편합니다.

> Last time I had a boyfriend, I felt I didn't have much of my personal life. Now I feel comfortable being alone.
>
> In my previous relationship, I felt I didn't have much personal freedom. These days, I'm at ease being by myself.
>
> My last relationship made me feel like my personal life was lacking. Now, I feel content being on my own.

'Last time + 주어 + 동사'는 '지난번에 ~했을 때'라는 뜻입니다. last time 앞에 전치사는 필요없죠. alone, by myself, on my own 모두 같은 의미입니다.

• **지난번에 남자 친구 사귈 때**
last time I had a boyfriend = in my previous relationship = my last relationship

• **혼자인 게 편하다**
comfortable being alone = at ease being by myself = content being on my own

---

A Last time I had a boyfriend I felt I didn't have much of my personal life. Now I feel comfortable being alone.
B Really? What made you feel that way?
A I think I was too focused on the relationship and neglected my own interests.

A 지난번에 남자친구 사귀었을 때는 개인의 삶이 없다고 느꼈어요. 지금은 혼자 있는 게 좋아요.
B 정말요? 왜 그렇게 느꼈어요?
A 남자친구 사귀는 데 너무 집중해서 제 관심사를 소홀히 했던 것 같아요.

48 지금 남자친구와의 관계에 대해 진지하게 생각하지 않아요. 함께 있는 것이 좋을 뿐이고, 그 이상 별로 생각하지 않습니다.

> I don't think seriously about relationship. I just love being together with him and don't think much other than that.
>
> I don't take our relationship too seriously. I just enjoy being with him and don't overthink it.
>
> I don't put much thought into the relationship. I just enjoy his company and keep things simple.

두번째 문장의 take ~ seriously는 ~을 진지하게 받아들인다는 뜻입니다. 세번째 문장의 company는 '회사'가 아니라 어떤 사람과 함께 있는 상황을 일컫습니다.

> • ~을 진지하게 생각하지 않는다
> not think seriously about ~ = not take ~ too seriously = not put much thought into ~
>
> • 함께 있는 것이 좋다
> love being together = enjoy being with him = enjoy his company

A I don't think seriously about relationship. I just love being together with her and don't think much other than that.
B I understand. Sometimes it's good to just enjoy the moment and not overthink things.

A 우리 관계에 대해 심각하게 생각하지 않아요. 그냥 함께 있는 게 좋고, 그 외에는 별로 생각하지 않아요.
B 이해 가요. 가끔은 그 순간을 즐기고 너무 많은 생각을 하지 않는 게 좋죠.

건강

49 제가 단 것을 너무 좋아하는데, 건강을 위해 줄여야겠어요.

> I love sweet foods too much. I need to reduce taking sugar.
>
> I have a huge weakness for sweet foods. I really need to cut down on my sugar intake.
>
> I enjoy sugary foods way too much. I should work on reducing my sugar consumption.

단 것은 sweet foods 혹은 sweets라고만 해도 됩니다. 두번째 문장은 '나는 단 것에 너무 취약하다' 정도 뜻이죠. '섭취'는 intake도 좋고, consumption이라고 해도 됩니다. consumption은 '소비'와 '섭취'를 모두 의미하죠. reduce를 구동사로 표현하면 cut down on입니다. on까지 잊지 말고 기억해야 하죠.

- **단 것을 좋아하다**
love sweet foods = have a huge weakness for sweet foods = enjoy sugary foods

- **설탕 섭취를 줄이다**
reduce taking sugar = cut down on my sugar intake = reducing my sugar consumption

A How's your diet going?
B I have a huge weakness for sweet foods. I really need to cut down on my sugar intake.
A They're my biggest temptation, too.

A 다이어트는 어떻게 되어 가고 있나요?
B 저는 단 음식에 너무 약해요. 설탕 섭취를 줄여야 합니다.
A 저의 가장 큰 유혹이기도 하죠.

50 건강이 중요하지만, 먹고 싶은 건 먹으며 인생을 즐기려 합니다.

> I know health is very important, but I'd rather eat what I want to eat and do what I want to do and have fun in my life.
>
> I understand health is crucial, but I'd choose to eat my favorite foods and live my life.
>
> Although I know health is important, I'd rather indulge in the foods I love and have fun in life.

세번째 문장의 indulge in은 어떤 것을 즐기거나 뭔가에 탐닉하는 태도를 일컫습니다. 인생을 즐기는 태도를 두번째 문장에서는 live my life라고 표현했죠. 내가 살고 싶은 인생을 산다는 뜻입니다.

> **• 먹고 싶은 걸 먹다**
> eat what I want to eat = eat my favorite foods = indulge in the foods I love

A How do you balance enjoying your favorite foods with staying healthy?
B I understand health is crucial, but I'd prefer to eat what I like and enjoy doing what makes me happy.
A Yeah. It's important to find joy in life.

A 좋아하는 음식을 즐기는 것과 건강을 유지하는 것 사이에서 어떻게 균형을 잡으시나요?
B 건강이 중요하다는 것은 알지만, 좋아하는 것을 먹고 나를 행복하게 하는 일을 즐기는 걸 더 선호해요.
A 맞아요. 인생에서 즐거움을 찾는 것이 중요하죠.

건강

51 패스트푸드, 인스턴트 식품은 건강에 안 좋잖아요. 줄여야겠어요.

> I know eating fast foods and instant foods is bad for health. I need to cut down on them.
>
> I'm aware that fast food and instant meals are unhealthy. I need to reduce my consumption of them.
>
> Fast food and instant meals are harmful to my health. I need to limit how much I eat them.

건강에 좋으면 healthy, 건강에 나쁘면 unhealthy로 표현할 수 있습니다. 안 좋은 음식을 줄인다고 할 때는 reduce, cut down on외에 limit을 활용해도 좋죠. 제한한다는 의미입니다.

- **건강에 안 좋다**
bad for health = unhealthy = harmful to my health

A It's important to be mindful of what we eat.
B Yes. Fast foods and instant meals are bad for health. I need to limit how much I eat them.
A I know. It's just so convenient sometimes, but we need to make better choices.

A 먹는 음식에 신경 써야 합니다.
B 예. 패스트푸드와 인스턴트식품은 건강에 해롭죠. 이런 음식은 제한적으로 먹어야 해요.
A 맞아요. 아주 편리할 때도 있지만, 더 나은 선택을 해야 하죠.

52 건강 보조식품 무시했는데, 꾸준히 먹으니 확실히 좋네요.

I didn't believe in health supplements, but I can feel the difference now after eating them for a while.

I was skeptical about health supplements, but after taking them for some time, I can feel the positive effects.

Initially, I didn't trust health supplements, but after a period of taking them, I notice a difference.

첫번째 문장의 believe in은 효능을 믿는다는 말입니다. 어떤 사람이나 그 사람이 한 말을 믿는다는 뜻의 believe와 차이가 있죠. '회의적이다'라는 뜻의 skeptical을 활용하여 효과를 의심한다는 의미를 전달할 수도 있죠.

• 건강 보조식품을 무시하다
not believe in health supplements = skeptical about health supplements = not trust health supplements

A I was skeptical about health supplements, but after taking them for some time, I can feel the positive effects.
B That's great to hear. It's always nice when something actually works.
A Yeah, I'm glad I gave them a try.

A 건강 보조 식품에 대해 회의적이었는데, 한동안 먹어 보니 긍정적인 효과가 느껴지네요.
B 좋네요. 뭐든 효과가 있으면 좋죠.
A 네, 시도해 보길 잘했어요.

건강

53 이제 건강에 신경 쓸 나이가 된 것 같습니다.

> Now I'm at an age when I need to pay more attention to my health.
>
> I'm at the point in life where I need to focus more on my health.
>
> I've come to a stage in life where health needs to be a higher priority.

'나이'는 정확한 '시점'을 말하므로 전치사 at과 함께 at an age라고 해야 적절합니다. 세번째 문장에서는 건강의 우선순위가 높아진다는 의미에서 higher priority를 활용하고 있죠. 우선순위가 더 높은 일에 더 많은 신경을 쓰게 되므로 이 문맥에서 적절한 표현입니다.

• ~할 나이가 되었다
be at an age when = be at the point in life where = come to a stage in life where

• 건강에 신경 쓰다
pay more attention to my health = focus more on my health
= health needs to be a higher priority

A I'm planning to eat healthier and exercise more regularly.
B Yeah, we're at an age when we need to pay more attention to our health.

A 더 건강하게 먹고 더 규칙적으로 운동할 계획입니다.
B 그래요. 우리도 이제 건강에 더 관심을 기울여야 할 나이가 되었죠.

54 먹는 게 중요하다고들 해서 건강한 음식을 먹으려 노력합니다.

> As they say, you are what you eat. That's why I try to eat healthy foods as much as possible.
>
> The popular saying, "You are what you eat," inspires me to eat healthy foods whenever I can.
>
> Because it's true that you are what you eat, I do my best to prioritize healthy eating.

'네가 먹는 것이 곧 너이다', '네가 먹는 것이 곧 네가 된다'로 직역할 수 있는 You are what you eat.은 음식의 중요성을 강조할 때 널리 쓰이는 표현입니다. 두번째 문장의 inspire는 자신감이나 열정을 지니게 만든다는 뜻입니다. '영감을 주다'라고만 이해하면 의미의 폭이 너무 좁아집니다.

• 건강한 음식을 먹다
eat healthy foods = prioritize healthy eating

- **A** How do you manage to stay healthy with such a busy schedule?
- **B** As they say, you are what you eat. That's why I try to eat healthy foods as much as possible.
- **A** That's a good approach. What kind of healthy foods do you like?

- **A** 일정이 그렇게 바쁜데 어떻게 건강을 유지하세요?
- **B** 먹는 게 중요하다고들 하잖아요. 그래서 가능한 한 건강한 음식을 먹으려고 합니다.
- **A** 좋은 자세네요. 건강에 좋은 음식 어떤 걸 좋아하세요?

건강

55 건강비결은 단순하죠. 잘 먹고 운동하는 건데, 지키기가 힘듭니다.

The secret to good health is simple. Eat healthy and exercise. The thing is it's hard to put into action.

The key to good health is straightforward: eat healthy and exercise. However, it's difficult to follow through.

Achieving good health is simple in theory: eat well and stay active. The hard part is actually doing it.

건강에 좋은 음식을 먹는 것을 eat healthy라고 표현합니다. 문법적으로 분석할 필요 없이 정해진 표현으로 기억하는 게 좋죠. 실천한다는 뜻의 기본 표현은 put ~ into action인데, 두번째 문장의 follow through도 유용합니다. 약속을 이행하거나 결심을 실천한다는 뜻이죠.

- **잘 먹고 운동한다**
  eat healthy and exercise = eat well and stay active

- **실천하다**
  put into action = follow through = actually do it

A The key to good health is straightforward: eat healthy and exercise. However, it's difficult to follow through.
B Yes, I try to eat balanced meals and work out regularly, but it's not always easy.
A 건강 비결은 단순합니다. 건강한 식습관과 운동이죠. 하지만 지키기가 어려워요.
B 네. 균형 잡힌 식사를 하고 규칙적으로 운동하려고 노력하지만 쉽지만은 않아요.

56 건강하려면 스트레스 관리가 정말 중요하죠. 평소에 어떻게 스트레스를 푸세요?

> Managing stress is really important for good health. How do you usually relieve stress?
>
> Taking care of stress is crucial for overall well-being. How do you typically deal with stress?
>
> Stress management plays a vital role in staying healthy. How do you de-stress?

스트레스를 해소한다고 할 때 쓰는 동사는 reduce, relieve, release입니다. relieve stress처럼 말하지 않고 de-stress라는 단어만 쓰기도 하죠. 동사에 접두사 de-를 붙이면 반대나 박탈을 의미합니다. 비활성화한다는 뜻인 deactivate, 삼림을 없앤다는 뜻인 deforest 등이 그 예입니다. 외래어 '웰빙'은 남용되는 경향이 있는데, 원래 영어표현 well-being은 '건강한 상태'를 말합니다.

- 건강
good health = well-being = staying healthy

- 스트레스를 풀다
relieve stress = deal with stress = de-stress

A Managing stress is really important for good health. How do you de-stress?
B When I chat and laugh with my friends, all my stress goes away!

A 건강하려면 스트레스 관리가 정말 중요하죠. 평소에 어떻게 스트레스를 푸세요?
B 친구들이랑 수다 떨면서 웃고 나면 스트레스가 다 사라져요!

용모

57 그 색깔 잘 어울리네요.

You look great in that color.

Wow, that color really suits you.

You are stunning in that color.

잘 어울린다고 할 때는 동사 suit을 활용할 수 있죠. 특히 옷이 잘 어울린다고 할 때도 적절한 동사입니다. 세번째 문장의 stunning은 '놀라게 하는'이라는 뜻이죠. 놀랍게 느껴질 정도로 좋거나 뛰어난 것을 가리키는 말로 쓰입니다.

> • 그 색이 잘 어울리다
> look great in that color = that color suits you = be stunning in that color

A Did you get a new shirt? That color really suits you.
B Thank you! I wasn't sure about it at first.
A It looks great on you. You should wear that color more often.

A 새 셔츠예요? 그 색 정말 잘 어울리네요.
B 고맙습니다! 처음에는 확신이 안 서더라고요.
A 잘 어울려요. 그 색을 더 자주 입으세요.

58 머리 자르셨군요. 짧게 자르니 더 어려 보이네요.

You had a haircut. You look younger with that shorter hair.

You got your hair cut! You look so much younger.

Hey, you got your hair done! I feel like shorter hair can take years off a person's face.

'머리를 자르다'는 명사 haircut으로 표현해도 되고, get somebody's hair cut처럼 소위 5형식 문형으로 표현할 수도 있습니다. cut 자리에 do를 넣어도 '머리를 하다'라는 뜻이 되죠. 세번째 문장의 take years off a person's face는 '얼굴에서 나이를 몇 년 덜어 낸다', 즉 어려 보이게 만든다는 뜻입니다.

• 머리를 자르다
had a haircut = got your hair cut = got your hair done

• 어려 보이다
look younger = take years off a person's face

A You had a haircut! You look younger with that shorter hair.
B Thank you! I wanted to try something different.
A It suits you. It really brings out your features.

A 머리 잘랐군요. 짧게 자르니 더 어려 보이네요.
B 고맙습니다. 새로운 시도를 해 보고 싶었어요.
A 잘 어울려요. 이목구비가 더 두드러져 보여요.

용모

59 저는 패션 감각이 없는 것 같아요.

I don't have much of a fashion sense.
I don't really have an eye for fashion.
I have no sense of style.

'패션 감각'은 '감각'에 해당하는 sense를 활용해 표현할 수 있습니다. have an eye for ~, have a talent for ~는 ~에 대한 감각이나 재능이 있다는 의미입니다.

> • 패션 감각이 없다
> not have much of a fashion sense = not have an eye for fashion = have no sense of style

A I don't have much of a fashion sense. I usually go for comfortable and casual clothes.
B No worries. Fashion can be tricky. Comfort is important.

A 저는 패션 감각이 별로 없어요. 그냥 편안하고 캐주얼한 옷을 즐겨 입는 편입니다.
B 걱정 마세요. 패션은 어려울 수 있어요. 편안한 게 중요하죠.

60 편하고 실용적인 옷을 좋아합니다.

I love clothes that are practical and make me feel comfortable.

I love practical and comfortable clothing.

I prefer practical clothing that feels comfy.

comfortable은 '편안한', practical은 '실용적'에 어울리는 단어죠. 구어에서는 comfortable을 comfy로 줄여 표현하기도 합니다.

> • 편하고 실용적인
> that are practical and make me feel comfortable = practical and comfortable = be practical and feel comfy

A I love clothes that are practical and make me feel comfortable.
B That's a good approach. Comfort is so important in daily wear.
A Exactly. I always look for clothes that I can wear all day without feeling restricted.

A 저는 실용적이고 편안한 옷을 좋아합니다.
B 좋은 생각이에요. 일상복에서 편안함은 매우 중요하죠.
A 맞아요. 저는 항상 답답하지 않고 하루 종일 입을 수 있는 옷을 찾아요.

용모

61 저는 패션에 관심이 많습니다. 옷이 날개라고 생각해요.

I'm so interested in fashion and think that clothes make the man.

I'm quite passionate about fashion. We do tend to judge books by their covers, after all!

I love fashion, and I really think that you are what you wear.

Clothes make the man.은 '옷이 날개다'에 해당하는 표현입니다. Don't judge a book by its cover(책 표지로 책을 평가하지 말라).라는 속담에서 not을 빼면 겉모습이 중요하다는 말이 되죠. 세번째 대안의 You are what you wear.는 '당신이 입는 옷이 곧 당신이 된다' 즉 '옷이 자신을 말해 준다'라는 뜻입니다.

- 패션에 관심이 있다

interested in fashion = passionate about fashion = love fashion

- 옷이 날개다

clothes make the man = judge books by their covers = you are what you wear

A Do you follow fashion trends?
B Yes, I'm really interested in fashion. I believe that clothes make the man.
A Awesome. Do you have a favorite fashion brand or designer?

A 패션 트렌드를 따르는 편인가요?
B 네, 저는 패션에 정말 관심이 많아요. 옷이 날개라고 생각해요.
A 멋지네요. 좋아하는 패션 브랜드나 디자이너가 있나요?

62 옷을 주로 어디서 사세요? 스타일이 좋아 보이셔서 여쭤봅니다.

> Where do you usually shop for clothes? Your style is great.
>
> You always look so stylish! Where do you get your outfits from?
>
> I love the way you dress! Do you have any favorite stores for clothes?

'스타일이 좋다'는 stylish라는 형용사 하나로 표현할 수도 있죠. 세번째 문장에서는 '당신이 옷을 입는 방식이 좋다'라고 달리 얘기하고 있습니다. 결국 스타일을 칭찬하는 표현이 되죠.

> • 스타일이 좋아 보인다
> your style is great = you look so stylish = I love the way you dress

A You always look so stylish! Where do you usually shop for clothes?
B Thanks so much! I love shopping at local boutiques and thrift stores.

A 항상 스타일리시해 보이시네요! 보통 어디서 옷을 사시나요?
B 고맙습니다! 집 근처 부티크와 중고품 매장에서 쇼핑하는 걸 좋아해요.

Exercise 1

다음 중 의미가 다른 문장 하나를 고르세요.

01

서울에서 나고 자랐습니다.

① I was born and grew up in Seoul.
② Since I was born, Seoul has truly become my second hometown.
③ Seoul is where I was born and brought up.
④ I was born and raised in Seoul.

02

최근에 이직했어요.

① I was recently given a pink slip.
② I recently got a new job.
③ I just started a new gig.
④ I just landed a new position.

03

오늘 일 정말 많았어요.

① It was a long day.
② I was swamped today.
③ I was buried under a pile of work today.
④ The day went by without a hitch.

04

끝이 보이니 조금 더 힘을 내야죠.

① The light at the end of the tunnel is in sight.
② We're almost there. We can do it!
③ I can't see any solution on the horizon
④ Just a little bit longer, and we can put this all behind us.

05

이 후텁지근한 날씨 정말 못 견디겠어요.

① I can't stand this muggy weather.
② The air is very crisp all day long.
③ I hate humid weather. It's awful.
④ This swampy air is the worst!

06

오랜만에 만나서 좋았어요.

① It was great seeing you for the first time in a while.
② It's been great to finally catch up with you!
③ It was wonderful to finally see you!
④ It's easy to lose touch with each other, right?

07

둘이 얼마나 사귀었나요?

① How long have you two been together?
② Have you guys been together for a while?
③ How much time has passed since your breakup?
④ How long have you both been in a relationship?

08

키 크고 잘생긴 남자를 좋아합니다.

① I love guys who are tall and good-looking.
② A man's appearance doesn't matter much to me.
③ Tall, dark, and handsome does it for me.
④ I'm into guys who are physically attractive.

09

남자친구와 서로 말이 잘 통해서 좋습니다.

① My boyfriend and I are at each other's throat.
② I love my boyfriend because we can talk a lot of things together.
③ My boyfriend and I are always on the same page.
④ I love my boyfriend because we communicate so well.

10

단 것을 너무 좋아해요.

① I love sweet foods too much.
② I have a huge weakness for sweet foods.
③ I have a sweet tooth.
④ I prefer savory foods over sweet ones.

11

그 색깔이 잘 어울리는 것 같습니다.

① You look great in that color.
② That color isn't flattering on you.
③ Wow, that color really suits you.
④ You are stunning in that color.

Exercise 1 정답 및 해설

01
어떤 장소에서 나고 자랐다고 할 때 쓰는 가장 일반적인 표현이 be born and raised in ~ 입니다. be raised 대신 성장한다는 뜻의 grow up, 역시 양육된다는 뜻의 be brought up 을 써도 좋죠. 2번의 second hometown은 '제2의 고향'이라는 의미이므로 뜻이 조금 다릅니다.

02
1번의 be given a pink slip 혹은 get a pink slip은 해고 통지를 받는다는 의미입니다. 해고 통지서가 핑크색이던 데서 유래한 표현이죠.

03
4번의 without a hitch는 '아무 문제 없이'라는 뜻입니다. 하루가 아무 문제 없이 잘 흘러 갔다는 뜻이 되므로 나머지 문장과 의미가 다릅니다.

04
3번의 on the horizon은 무언가가 수평선 혹은 지평선에 모습을 드러내는 것을 말합니다. 이제 막 시작되거나 모습을 드러낸다는 뜻인데, can't see any solution on the horizon 이라고 했으므로, 해결의 조짐이 보이지 않는다는 말이죠.

05
crisp는 바삭한 음식물을 묘사하거나 쾌청하고 건조한 날씨를 나타내는 형용사입니다. 습도가 많은 상황과는 반대이므로 답은 2번입니다.

06
누군가와 연락을 유지하는 것이 keep in touch with ~이고 그 반대말이 lose touch with 입니다. 4번은 '서로 연락이 끊어지기 쉽다'라는 말이므로 의미가 다릅니다.

07
남녀가 헤어지는 것을 breakup이라고 하죠. 3번은 '헤어진 지 얼마나 되었냐'라는 질문 입니다.

08
2번 문장은 '남자의 외모는 내게 그리 중요하지 않다'라는 말입니다. 외모가 중요하다는 나머지 세 문장과 반대되는 뜻이죠.

09
1번 문장의 at each other's throat은 직역하면 '서로의 목구멍 안에 있다'인데, 서로 심한 갈등 관계임을 묘사하는 이디엄입니다. 나머지 세 문장과 정반대의 뜻이죠.

10
3번의 have a sweet tooth는 단 것을 좋아한다는 뜻의 관용 표현입니다. 4번의 savory는 천연의 풍부한 맛을 묘사하는 형용사이죠. 결국 '인공적인 단맛을 싫어한다'는 말이므로 다른 세 문장과 의미가 다릅니다.

11
flatter는 '아부하다'라는 뜻 외에 '근사하게 보이게 만들다'라는 의미도 지닙니다. flattering하지 않다고 말했으므로 잘 어울리지 않는다는 뜻이고, 나머지 문장들과 의미가 다릅니다.

정답 1.② 2.① 3.④ 4.③ 5.② 6.④ 7.③ 8.② 9.① 10.④ 11.②

좋은 것을 말하는 스몰토크

취미
운동
맛집, 음식
여행
쇼핑
반려동물
Exercise 2

취미

63 어떤 취미가 있으세요?

So, what do you do for fun?

So, any hobbies?

What do you like to do for fun?

'취미'는 영어로 hobby이지만, 일상에서는 do something for fun처럼 표현하는 경우도 잦습니다. 재미로 하는 일이 취미이기 때문이죠.

> • 취미가 있다
> do ~ for fun = hobbies = like to do ~ for fun

A So, what do you do for fun?
B I love playing basketball. It's a great way to stay active and hang out with friends. How about you?
A I'm really into tennis these days. My skills have improved a lot with regular practice.

A 어떤 취미 있으세요?
B 농구하는 걸 좋아해요. 몸을 움직이면서 친구들과 어울리기에도 좋죠. 취미 있으세요?
A 요즘 테니스에 빠져 있어요. 규칙적으로 연습하니 실력이 많이 향상됐어요.

64 주말에 보통 뭐 하세요?

> How do you fill time on the weekends?
> How do you spend your time on the weekends?
> What do you do on your downtime?

세번째 문장의 downtime은 '일하지 않는 시간'을 말합니다. 일하지 않는 주말에 무슨 일을 하냐는 질문이므로 on your downtime이라고 해도 좋죠.

• 주말에 무언가를 하며 시간을 보내다

fill time on the weekends = spend time on the weekends = do something on one's downtime

---

A So, what do you do on your downtime?
B I love reading mystery novels and playing the guitar.
A That sounds fun! I enjoy cooking and trying out new recipes.

A 쉬는 날에는 무얼 하세요?
B 미스터리 소설 읽고 기타 치는 것을 좋아해요.
A 재밌을 것 같네요! 저는 요리하고 새로운 요리법을 시도해보는 걸 좋아해요.

취미

65 새로운 취미를 찾고 있습니다. 추천할 만한 것 있으신가요?

> I'm in the market for a new hobby. What do you like to do?
> I've been looking for a new hobby. Know any good ones?
> I'm thinking about starting a new hobby. Can you recommend any?

in the market은 '시장에서'라는 뜻 이외에 무언가를 찾고 있다는 의미도 지닙니다. 구입할 물건을 찾는다는 뜻만은 아니니, 오역하지 않도록 주의해야 합니다.

> • 새로운 취미를 찾고 있다
> be in the market for a new hobby = look for a new hobby = think about starting a new hobby

A I'm in the market for a new hobby. What do you like to do?
B I love gardening. It's so relaxing and rewarding to see your plants grow. Have you ever tried it?
A Not really, but it sounds interesting.

A 새로운 취미를 찾고 있어요. 뭐 하는 걸 좋아하세요?
B 화초 가꾸는 걸 좋아해요. 화초들이 자라는 걸 보고 있으면 편안하고 보람이 느껴져요. 화초 가꿔본 적 있으세요?
A 없지만 재미있을 것 같네요.

66 저도 그거 해 봤는데. 저한테는 안 맞더라고요.

> I tried that hobby, but it wasn't my cup of tea.
> I have tried that, but it didn't really suit me.
> I've given that a go, but it wasn't really my thing.

시도해 보는 것은 한 단어로 try라고 하면 되고, give a shot/go/try라고 표현할 수도 있습니다. 나한테는 안 어울린다는 의미를 전달하는 방법도 다양한데, not my cup of tea라는 관용 표현도 있고, 간단히 not my thing이라고 할 수도 있습니다.

> • 나한테는 안 맞는다
> not my cup of tea = not really suit me = not really my thing

A I tried that hobby, but it wasn't my cup of tea.
B Really? What didn't you like about it?
A I just couldn't get into it. It didn't hold my interest like I thought it would.

A 그 취미 시도해봤지만, 내 취향이 아니었어요.
B 그래요? 어떤 게 마음에 들지 않았어요?
A 그냥 별로 좋아지지 않았어요. 생각했던 만큼 흥미롭지 않더군요.

취미

67 돈이 문제가 안 된다면 어떤 취미 가져보고 싶으세요?

If money were no object, what hobby would you have?

If you didn't have to worry about money, what would you do for a hobby?

If you were super-rich, what hobby would you pick up?

'금전적인 제한이 없다면'이라고 할 때 쓰는 거의 정해진 표현이 if money were no object입니다. 실제로 그렇기는 힘들고 가정해서 얘기하는 것이므로 be 동사는 were를 씁니다. 세번째 문장의 pick up은 바닥에서 줍는다는 의미 외에, 선택하거나 습관을 들인다는 뜻도 지닙니다.

> • 돈이 문제가 안 된다
> money is no object = not have to worry about money = be super-rich

A If money were no object, what hobby would you have?
B I think I would travel the world and explore different cultures. How about you?
A I'd probably take up yachting. There's something so freeing about being out on the open water.

A 돈이 문제가 되지 않는다면 어떤 취미를 가져 보고 싶으세요?
B 전 세계를 여행하며 다양한 문화를 탐험하고 싶어요. 어떤 취미 가져보고 싶으세요?
A 요트를 타보려고요. 탁 트인 바다에 나가면 해방감을 느낄 수 있잖아요.

68 최근에 라인댄스를 시작했는데, 정말 재밌어요.

I recently started line-dancing, and that's a really fun hobby for me.

I just started line-dancing. I'm having a great time with it.

I recently picked up line-dancing. I'm really enjoying it.

세번째 문장의 pick up은 앞서 설명한 것처럼 '선택'이나 '습관'을 나타냅니다.

- 최근에 ~을 시작했다
recently started = just started = recently picked up

A I recently started line-dancing, and it's such a fun hobby for me.
B I've always wanted to try line-dancing. Is it difficult to learn?
A Not at all! The steps are pretty simple once you get the hang of it. Plus, it's a great way to meet new people.

A 최근에 라인 댄스를 시작했는데, 정말 재밌는 취미예요.
B 저도 항상 해보고 싶었어요. 배우기 어렵나요?
A 전혀요! 한번 익숙해지면 발동작이 꽤 간단해요. 새로운 사람들도 만날 수 있는 좋은 방법이에요.

운동

69 헬스 끊어 놓고 안 간 지 한 달이 넘었어요.

I signed up for the gym, but I haven't been there for longer than a month.

I joined the gym, but it's been over a month since I last went.

I haven't been to the gym in over a month since I signed up.

헬스클럽은 gym(체육관)이라고 해야 자연스럽습니다. 헬스클럽 등 어떤 프로그램에 등록하는 것은 sign up이라고 하죠. '마지막으로 간 후 안 갔다'는 의미를 강조하기 위해 두번째 문장에서는 last를 넣었습니다.

- **헬스 끊다**
sign up for the gym = join the gym

- **한 달 넘게 안 가다**
haven't been there for longer than a month = over a month since I last went = haven't been to the gym in over a month

A I signed up for the gym, but I haven't been there for longer than a month.
B I can relate to that. It's hard to stay consistent.
A The gym membership is not cheap, either!

A 헬스 끊고 한 달 넘게 못 갔어요.
B 이해가 가요. 꾸준히 하기가 힘들잖아요.
A 헬스비가 저렴하지도 않은데 말이죠.

70 요즘 배가 나와서 헬스를 끊었어요.

> I gain belly fat these days, so I signed up for the gym.
>
> I've been putting on belly fat lately, so I joined the gym.
>
> I signed up for the gym because I've been gaining weight around my belly recently.

배에 생기는 지방, 즉 뱃살은 belly fat이라고 합니다. sign up for the gym 대신 join the gym이라고 해도 헬스클럽에 등록한다는 뜻이 되죠.

> • 배가 나오다
> gain belly fat = put on belly fat = gain weight around my belly

A I've been putting on belly fat lately, so I joined the gym.
B Great. It will definitely help you get back in shape.
A Yeah. I'm trying a mix of cardio and strength.

A 요즘 뱃살이 많이 늘어서 헬스 끊었어요.
B 좋아요. 예전 모습을 회복하는 데 도움이 될 거예요.
A 네. 유산소 운동과 근력 운동을 병행하고 있어요.

운동

71 일주일에 3회 이상, 한 번에 30분 이상 유산소 운동을 해야 합니다.

> You're supposed to do aerobic exercise longer than 30 minutes, more than three times a week.
>
> You should do cardio for over 30 minutes, at least three times a week.
>
> Performing aerobic exercise for more than half an hour, three times a week, is advised.

'에어로빅'이라는 말이 익숙하지만, 원래 aerobic은 유산소 운동을 가리키는 단어입니다. 달리 cardio라고도 하는데, 원래 cardio는 '심장'과 관련된 것을 표현하는 접두사죠. 심장이 뛰게 만드는 운동, 즉 유산소 운동을 말할 때 활용합니다.

- **유산소 운동을 하다**
  do aerobic exercise = do cardio = perform aerobic exercises

A I've been trying to get back into shape, but it's hard to stay motivated.
B You are recommended to do cardio for over 30 minutes, at least three times a week.
A Yeah. The key is to keep your heart rate up, right?

A 다시 예전 몸매를 되찾으려고 노력하는데, 계속 열심히 하기가 힘드네요.
B 일주일에 최소 3회, 30분 이상씩 유산소 운동을 하는 것이 좋아요.
A 네. 심박수를 높이는 게 가장 중요한 거잖아요.

72 운동할 시간을 따로 내지 않고, 엘리베이터 대신 계단을 이용하려 노력합니다.

> Instead of taking time to work out, I try to walk stairs and don't use an elevator.
>
> Instead of setting aside time to exercise, I choose to take the stairs rather than the elevator.
>
> Rather than dedicating time to working out, I make an effort to use stairs over the elevator.

'운동하다'는 exercise 혹은 work out으로 표현하면 됩니다. 시간을 낸다고 할 때 특히 두번째 문장의 set aside가 유용하죠. 따로 떼어 놓는다는 뜻입니다.

• 계단을 이용하다
walk stairs = take the stairs = use stairs

• 운동할 시간을 내다
take time to work out = set aside time to exercise = dedicate time to working out

---

A Instead of setting aside time to exercise, I choose to take the stairs rather than the elevator.
B That's a smart idea. Small changes can make a big difference.
A Exactly. It's an easy way to add some physical activity to my daily routine.

A 운동할 시간을 내는 대신, 엘리베이터보다는 계단을 이용하고 있어요.
B 좋은 생각이네요. 작은 변화가 큰 차이를 만들 수 있잖아요.
A 맞아요. 일상 생활에 운동을 추가하는 쉬운 방법이죠.

운동

73 조깅을 시작했는데, 매일 뛰어요. 하루라도 안 뛰면 이상합니다.

> I started jogging, and now I run every day. If I skip a day, I feel like I'm missing something.
>
> I began jogging and now run daily. When I miss a day, I feel really restless.
>
> I got into jogging, and now it's a daily routine. Skipping a day makes me feel quite uncomfortable.

'하루라도 안 뛰면 이상하다'의 '이상하다'는 strange로 표현하기에는 부적절합니다. 뭔가 빠진 듯하고 어색하다는 의미이므로 missing something, restless(초조한), uncomfortable(불편한) 같은 표현들이 어울리죠.

> • 매일 뛴다
> run every day = run daily = jogging is a daily routine
>
> • (하던 걸 안 하면) 이상하다
> feel like I'm missing something = feel restless = feel uncomfortable

A I began jogging and now run daily. When I miss a day, I feel really restless.
B It's great that you've found something that works so well for you.
A Yeah. It helps clear my mind and keeps me in good shape.

A 조깅을 시작했고 매일 달리기를 하고 있습니다. 하루라도 안 하면 이상해요.
B 자신에게 잘 맞는 것을 찾게 되었다니 좋네요.
A 네. 마음을 맑게 하고 몸을 건강히 유지하는 데 도움이 됩니다.

74 이 피트니스 앱을 이용해서 운동한 내역을 체크하고 있어요. 추천합니다.

> I've been using this fitness app to track my workouts and progress. I recommend it.
>
> I use this fitness app to monitor my workouts and progress. It's worth trying.
>
> Using this fitness app has really helped me stay on top of my workouts. I'd recommend giving it a try.

운동한 내역을 체크하고 기록하는 것은 track(추적하다), monitor(모니터링하다)와 같은 동사로 표현할 수 있죠. 세번째 문장의 stay on top of ~는 어떤 것을 완전히 통제하고 잘 알고 있다는 의미입니다. 내가 운동한 내역을 상세히 알게 해준다는 의미로 쓴 표현이죠.

• 운동한 내역을 체크하다
track my workouts = monitor my workouts = stay on top of my workouts

---

A I keep hearing about fitness apps. Do you use one?
B Yeah, I do! I've been using this fitness app to track my workouts and progress. I recommend it.

A 요즘 피트니스 앱에 대한 얘기 많이 듣게 되던데, 혹시 쓰는 거 있으세요?
B 네, 사용해요. 이 피트니스 앱을 사용해서 운동 내역과 진행 상황을 추적하고 있어요. 추천합니다.

맛집, 음식

75 매운 음식을 좋아합니다.

> I love spicy food.
>
> Spicy food is my favorite.
>
> I never say no to spicy food!

매운 고추 등을 표현하는 hot과 달리, 양념으로 인해 맵게 느껴지는 경우 spicy로 표현하죠. 세번째 문장의 never say no to는 '싫다고 하지 않는다' 즉 좋아한다는 뜻입니다.

- **(특정 음식을) 좋아한다**
  love = be my favorite = never say no to

A Do you have any favorite types of cuisine?
B Spicy food is my favorite.
A What kind of spicy dishes do you like?
B I love anything with a good kick, but I especially enjoy spicy curries.

A 좋아하는 요리 있으세요?
B 매운 음식을 가장 좋아합니다.
A 어떤 매운 요리를 좋아하나요?
B 자극적인 건 다 좋아하지만, 특히 매운 카레를 좋아합니다.

76 거기 맛집이에요. 한 시간 이상 줄을 서서 먹는 집입니다.

The restaurant is very famous. You have to wait in line for longer than an hour.

The restaurant is really well-known. You'll probably wait for an hour to get in.

The restaurant is so hot right now. You have to wait an hour before you can sit down.

'맛집'을 가리키는 한 단어는 없고, 유명하다는 말을 붙여 표현하면 됩니다. 결국 식당에 들어가거나(get in) 자리를 잡기 위해(sit down) 줄을 서는 것이므로 두번째와 세번째 문장처럼 표현할 수 있죠.

> • 유명한
> famous = well-known = so hot
>
> • 한 시간 줄을 서서 기다리다
> wait in line for an hour = wait for an hour to get in = wait an hour before you can sit down

A I went to a new place downtown. The restaurant is very famous. I had to wait in line for longer than an hour.
B Wow, that's a long wait. Was the food worth it?
A Absolutely. The dishes were incredible.

A 시내에 새로 생긴 식당에 갔어요. 맛집인데, 한 시간 이상 줄을 서야 했어요.
B 와, 정말 오래 기다렸네요. 음식이 그만큼 좋았나요?
A 물론이요. 음식이 정말 훌륭했어요.

맛집, 음식

77 태국 음식 드셔 보셨나요?

Have you ever tried Thai food?

Have you ever experienced Thai food?

Is this your first time having Thai food?

try는 시도하거나 경험하거나 먹어보는 것 모두를 표현할 수 있습니다. 세번째 문장처럼 Is this your first time -ing?라고 말하면 ~을 처음 해보냐는 말이 되죠.

> • 음식을 먹어 보다
> try = experience = have

A Have you ever experienced Thai food?
B Yes, I have. I love the balance of sweet, salty, sour, and spicy in their dishes.

A 태국 음식 드셔본 적 있나요?
B 네, 먹어봤어요. 단맛, 짠맛, 신맛, 매운맛이 균형을 이루는 게 좋았어요.

78 거기 음식은 맛있는데 가격이 너무 비싸요.

> I think the food there is good, but it's over-priced.
>
> The food is all right but not worth the price.
>
> I think the food is okay, but they charge way too much.

expensive 말고 비싸다는 뜻을 표현하는 방법은 다양합니다. over-를 붙여 가격이 너무 높다고 할 수도 있고, 두번째처럼 '그 정도 가격의 가치가 없다'라고 해도 되죠. 세번째 문장의 charge는 비용을 청구한다는 뜻입니다.

> • 가격이 비싸다
> over-priced = not worth the price = charge way too much

A Have you tried the new restaurant downtown? I've heard mixed reviews about it.
B Yes, I went there last weekend. I think the food there is good, but it's over-priced.

A 시내에 새로 생긴 식당 가보셨나요? 평가가 엇갈리던데요.
B 네, 지난 주말에 갔어요. 음식은 맛있지만 가격이 너무 비싼 것 같았어요.

맛집, 음식

79 이 근처에 추천할 식당이 있나요?

Can you recommend any good restaurants in this area?

Do you know any good restaurants around here?

Is there anywhere nearby to get a bite to eat?

세번째 문장의 get a bite to eat은 '먹다'라는 뜻의 구어 표현입니다. bite가 한 입 무는 것을 가리키므로, '뭔가를 먹어 보다'라는 말이 되죠.

> • 추천할 식당이 있다
> recommend any good restaurants = know any good restaurants = anywhere nearby to get a bite to eat

A Can you recommend any good restaurants in this area?
B Absolutely! There's a nice Italian place called Bella Roma that's known for its delicious pasta dishes.

A 이 지역에 추천할 만한 식당 있나요?
B 물론입니다! 벨라 로마라고 이탈리아 레스토랑인데, 파스타가 맛있기로 유명합니다.

80 이 음식 처음 먹어 보는데 뒷맛이 아주 좋네요.

> This is my first time trying this food, and I love it. The aftertaste is great.
>
> This is my first taste of this food, and it's amazing. The aftertaste is fantastic.
>
> This is my first experience with this food, and I really like it! It's got a great aftertaste.

뒷맛은 aftertaste라고 합니다. 두번째 문장의 first taste는 '처음 맛보는 경험'이라는 뜻이죠.

> **• 이 음식 처음 먹어 본다**
> my first time trying = my first taste of this food = my first experience with this food

A It was my first experience with Tagine, and I really liked it! It's got a great aftertaste.
B Then, it's on my list to try.

A 타진을 처음 먹어봤는데 정말 맛있었어요! 뒷맛이 훌륭해요.
B 그럼 저도 먹어 볼 요리 목록에 올려두겠습니다.

맛집, 음식

81 느끼한 음식 좋아합니다.

> I love foods that are cheesy.
> All my favorite foods are fatty.
> I really love oily foods.

느끼한 음식을 oily라고 해도 좋지만, 보통 치즈가 많이 들어가서 느끼한 음식은 cheesy, 육즙이 많아 느끼한 고기류의 음식은 fatty라고 표현합니다.

> • (음식이) 느끼한
> cheesy = fatty = oily

A I love foods that are cheesy.
B Me too! I could eat macaroni and cheese every day.
A I really enjoy pizza with extra cheese and cheesy nachos.

A 저는 치즈가 들어간 음식을 좋아해요.
B 저도요! 저는 마카로니 앤 치즈를 매일 먹을 수 있어요.
A 저는 치즈가 많이 들어간 피자와 치즈 나초를 정말 좋아해요.

82 요즘엔 안 먹어 본 음식이 먹어보고 싶네요.

I've been craving something new lately.

I feel like trying something different for a change.

I've been in the mood for something fresh.

crave는 우리말 '음식이 당기다'와 잘 어울리는 동사입니다. 어떤 음식이 먹고 싶다고 할 때 쓸 수 있죠. 달리 feel like trying ~, be in the mood for ~라고 해도 어떤 것을 하고 싶다는 의미가 됩니다. 두번째 문장의 for a change는 '기분 전환을 위해' 정도 뜻입니다.

> • 새로운 음식이 먹어보고 싶다
> crave something new = feel like trying something different = be in the mood for something fresh

A I've been craving something new lately.
B Same here! How about something spicy like Indian or Thai cuisine?
A I've been wanting to try Ethiopian food. It sounds so unique!

A 요즘 새로운 음식이 먹어보고 싶던데요.
B 저도요! 인도나 태국 요리처럼 매콤한 건 어때요?
A 에티오피아 음식을 먹어보고 싶었어요. 정말 독특해 보이잖아요.

맛집, 음식

83 요리하는 것 좋아하고, 꽤 한다고 생각해요. 대부분 직접 요리해서 먹어요.

> I love cooking, and I think I'm pretty good at it. I cook for myself most of the time.
>
> I love to mess around in the kitchen, and I'm not half bad. I cook almost all of my own meals.
>
> I love cooking, and I think I do okay. I cook my own meals most days.

두번째 문장의 mess around는 다양한 의미를 지니는 구동사입니다. 바람을 피운다는 뜻도 지니고, 여기서는 어떤 장소에 있으면서 뭔가를 해본다는 뜻이죠. 실험적으로 시도해 본다는 뉘앙스를 지닙니다. '나쁘지 않다'를 not bad 라고 하는데, not half bad는 half가 들어갔으므로, not bad보다는 좀 더 좋다는 의미입니다.

> **• 꽤 잘 한다**
> I'm pretty good = I'm not half bad = I think I do okay

A I love cooking, and I think I'm pretty good at it. I cook for myself most of the time.
B That's fantastic. What's your favorite dish to make?
A I really enjoy making pasta dishes. There's so much you can do with them.

A 저는 요리하는 걸 좋아하고, 제법 잘 합니다. 거의 직접 해 먹어요.
B 대단하네요. 제일 좋아하는 요리는 뭐예요?
A 파스타 만드는 거 정말 좋아해요. 파스타로 할 수 있는 게 정말 많아요.

84 요리에 소질이 없어서 배달시켜 먹거나 즉석조리 식품을 먹어요.

> I don't think I have a talent for cooking. Most of the time I order out or buy frozen food.
>
> I don't think I have a knack for cooking. I usually order takeout or get frozen food from the store.
>
> I'm a pretty bad cook. I just can't seem to make anything work. I typically order delivery or buy frozen meals.

'음식을 배달시키다'는 order out이라고 합니다. 전자레인지에 데워 먹는 즉석 식품은 frozen food라고 하죠. have a talent for ~가 ~에 소질이 있다는 뜻이지만, 두번째 문장의 have a knack for ~도 ~에 능력이나 소질이 있다는 의미입니다.

- 요리에 소질이 없다
not have a talent for cooking = not have a knack for cooking
= be a pretty bad cook

- 음식을 배달시키다
order out = order takeout = order delivery

A I don't think I have a talent for cooking. Most of the time I order out or buy frozen food.
B That's okay. Cooking isn't for everyone. Do you have a favorite place to order from?
A Yes, there's a great Vietnamese restaurant nearby that I love.

A 저는 요리에 재능이 없는 것 같아요. 대부분 배달시키거나 냉동식품을 사요.
B 괜찮아요. 모두가 요리를 잘하는 건 아니잖아요. 자주 시켜먹는 곳 있나요?
A 네, 근처에 제가 좋아하는 베트남 식당이 있어요.

맛집, 음식

85 **아내가 요리를 아주 잘 합니다.**

> My wife is such a good cook.
>
> My wife is a fantastic chef.
>
> My wife's cooking is out of this world.

chef는 cook(요리사)을 가리키는 또 다른 표현이죠. 세번째 문장의 out of this world는 '이 세상 출신이 아니다'라고 직역할 수 있는데, 외계에서 왔다고 해도 좋을 만큼 능력이 뛰어나다고 할 때 쓰는 표현입니다.

> • 요리를 잘 하다
>
> be a good cook = be a fantastic chef = one's cooking is out of this world

A Do you enjoy home-cooked meals?
B Yes. Thankfully, my wife is such a good cook.
A You're lucky. What's her specialty?

A 집밥 좋아하시나요?
B 네. 감사하게도 제 아내가 요리를 정말 잘해요.
A 운이 좋으시네요. 어떤 요리를 특히 잘하세요?

86 멀리 있어도 맛집을 찾아 직접 가서 먹어보는 거 좋아해요.

> I love finding out and visiting famous restaurants even though they are located very far.
>
> I enjoy discovering and visiting renowned restaurants, even if they're far away.
>
> I love seeking out and traveling to famous restaurants, regardless of distance.

유명하다는 의미를 표현하는 단어에 famous 말고 renowned도 있죠. '맛집'은 famous restaurant, renowned restaurant 정도로 표현하면 적당합니다. 세번째 문장의 seek out은 뭔가를 열심히 찾거나 추구하는 모양을 표현합니다.

> • 맛집을 찾아서 가 보다
> find out and visit famous restaurants = discover and visit renowned restaurants = seek out and travel to famous restaurants

A I enjoy discovering and visiting renowned restaurants, even if they're far away.
B Same here. Last weekend, I went to a barbecue place in the next city. It was the best I've ever tasted.

A 저는 좀 멀리 있더라도 맛집을 찾아서 가 보는 것을 좋아합니다.
B 저도요. 지난 주말에 근처 도시에 있는 바베큐 식당에 갔어요. 제가 먹어본 것 중 최고였어요.

여행

87 유럽 국가 중에 어디 가보셨어요?

> Which European countries have you visited?
>
> Where in Europe have you been?
>
> Tell me everywhere you've been in Europe.

국가를 방문한다고 할 때 visit이라고 할 수 있지만, be동사를 활용해도 되죠. have been in, have been to의 형태로 방문한 경험을 물을 수 있습니다.

> • 방문하다
> visit = have been

A Which European countries have you visited?
B I've been to France, Italy, and Spain. Each one was amazing.
A Did you have a favorite among them?
B It's hard to choose, but I think Italy had the best food and scenery.

A 유럽 국가 중 어디 가보셨어요?
B 프랑스, 이탈리아, 스페인에 가봤어요. 다 좋았어요.
A 그 중에서 어떤 나라가 제일 좋았어요?
B 고르기 힘들지만, 이탈리아가 음식과 경치가 가장 좋았다고 생각해요.

88 방문한 국가 중 어디가 제일 좋았습니까?

> Which country did you like the most out of all the countries you ever visited?
>
> Out of all the countries you've been to, which was your favorite?
>
> Which one has been your favorite place to travel?

'모든 국가들 중에서'는 out of all the countries와 같이 out of를 활용하여 표현하면 됩니다. 두번째 문장에서는 역시 have been to를 활용해서 방문한 적이 있다는 의미를 나타내고 있죠.

> **• 제일 좋았던 곳**
> like the most = be one's favorite = be one's favorite place to travel

A Out of all the countries you've been to, which was your favorite?
B It's hard to choose, but I think Japan was my favorite.
A What did you like most about it?
B The culture, the food, and the beautiful landscapes were all incredible.

A 방문했던 나라 중에서 어디가 제일 좋았어요?
B 고르기 힘들지만, 일본이 제일 좋았던 것 같아요.
A 가장 좋았던 점은 뭔가요?
B 문화, 음식, 아름다운 풍경이 모두 놀라웠어요.

여행

89 방문한 곳 중 어디가 가장 기억에 남습니까?

What's the most memorable place you've ever visited?

What place has impressed you the most?

Which place left the biggest impression on you?

기억에 남는 것은 memorable로 표현할 수 있습니다. '인상적이다'라고 해도 기억에 남는다는 뜻이므로 동사 impress 혹은 leave impression과 같은 표현을 활용할 수 있죠.

> • 가장 기억에 남는 곳
> the most memorable place = impress you the most = leave the biggest impression

A What's the most memorable place you've ever visited?
B I think it has to be Machu Picchu in Peru. The breathtaking views were unforgettable.
A That sounds incredible. I've always wanted to go there.

A 방문해 본 곳 중에 가장 기억에 남는 장소는 어디인가요?
B 페루의 마추픽추라고 생각해요. 숨 막힐 듯한 경치가 정말 기억에 남아요.
A 멋지네요. 제가 항상 가보고 싶은 곳이죠.

90 이번 여름에 어디 가시나요?

Are you going anywhere for the summer?

Do you have any summer vacation plans?

Anything fun planned for the summer?

우리말 '어디 가다'는 그대로 영어로 옮겨 go anywhere라고 하면 됩니다. 휴가계획을 말할 때도 plan을 활용할 수 있으므로, have plans 혹은 anything planned와 같이 표현할 수 있죠.

• 여름에 어디 가다

go anywhere for the summer = have summer vacation plans
= have anything fun planned for the summer

A Are you going anywhere for the summer?
B I'm thinking about taking a trip to Europe. How about you?
A I'm planning to visit my friend in Hawaii.

A 이번 여름에 어디 가세요?
B 유럽 여행을 갈까 고민 중이에요. 무슨 계획 있으세요?
A 하와이에 있는 친구를 방문할 계획이에요.

여행

91 유명 관광지도 좋지만, 그 지역의 특색을 느낄 수 있는 덜 알려진 곳을 방문하고 싶어요.

> Visiting famous tourist destinations is fine, but I'd love to visit relatively unknown areas where I can really feel the characteristics of the region.
>
> It's fine to see famous sights, but I'd love to get off the beaten path and enjoy some authentic local culture.
>
> There's nothing wrong with visiting common tourist destinations, but I'd rather poke around and see how the locals live.

off the beaten path에서 beaten은 때린다는 뜻인 beat의 과거분사인데, 발길이 이어져 닳았다는 말이죠. 그런 곳에서 벗어나는(off) 것이므로 발길이 뜸하다는 뜻입니다. poke around는 여기저기 가볍게 다녀 본다는 의미입니다.

• 유명 관광지
famous tourist destinations = famous sights = common tourist destinations

• 덜 알려진 곳에 가다
visit relatively unknown areas = get off the beaten path = poke around and see how the locals live

A It's fine to see famous sights, but I'd love to get off the beaten path and enjoy some authentic local culture.
B I know what you mean. The best experiences often come from exploring lesser-known places.

A 명소에 가 보는 것도 괜찮지만, 뻔한 여정에서 벗어나 고유한 지역 문화를 즐겨보고 싶어요.
B 무슨 말씀인지 이해가 가요. 덜 알려진 곳을 다니다가 최고의 경험을 하게 되는 경우가 있죠.

92 저는 야외 캠핑보다는 좋은 호텔에 머무는 게 더 좋습니다.

I prefer staying in a nice hotel than camping outdoors.

I'd rather stay in a comfy hotel than camp outdoors.

I prefer sleeping in a comfortable bed, rather than sleeping on the ground.

outdoors 단어 하나로 '야외'를 표현할 수 있죠. 캠핑을 하면 땅바닥에서 자게 되므로 세번째 문장처럼 표현할 수도 있습니다.

- 좋은 호텔에 머물다
stay in a nice hotel = stay in a comfy hotel = sleep in a comfortable bed

- 야외 캠핑을 하다
camp outdoors = sleep on the ground

A Do you enjoy spending time in nature?
B I do, but I prefer staying in a nice hotel than camping outdoors.
A I can understand that. Hotels offer more comfort and convenience.

A 자연에서 시간 보내는 것 좋아하시나요?
B 좋아하지만, 야외 캠핑보다 좋은 호텔에 머무는 것이 더 좋아요.
A 이해가 가요. 호텔이 더 편안하고 편리하잖아요.

여행

93 아이가 캠핑을 좋아해서 자주 가는 편입니다.

> My children love camping, so I try to go outdoors as often as possible.
>
> My children love sleeping in a tent, so I try to go camping as often as possible.
>
> My kids love camping, so we try to get away from civilization as much as we can.

go camping, go outdoors 대신 세번째 문장에서는 get away from civilization이라고 했습니다. 직역하면 '문명에서 벗어나다'인데, 도심에서 벗어나는 것을 말합니다.

- 캠핑을 가다
go outdoors = go camping = get away from civilization

A My children love camping, so I try to go outdoors as often as possible.
B That's great. It's wonderful to share those experiences with your kids.
A It really is. They have so much fun exploring nature.

A 저희 아이들이 캠핑을 좋아해서 가능한 한 자주 야외로 나가려 합니다.
B 멋지네요. 아이들과 함께 경험하는 건 정말 근사한 일이에요.
A 정말 그래요. 아이들은 자연을 탐험하는 걸 정말 좋아하잖아요.

94 해외도 좋지만 국내에도 아직 안 가본 좋은 곳이 많아요.

I love traveling overseas, but I know there are many great places to visit inside Korea, too.

I enjoy traveling abroad, but I'm also aware that Korea has many wonderful places to visit.

Traveling to foreign countries is my passion, but I know there are plenty of fantastic destinations within Korea as well.

overseas나 abroad 모두 외국을 표현하는 부사로 쓰입니다. 세번째 문장에 쓰인 ~ is my passion은 ~을 좋아하거나 열정적으로 한다는 뜻으로 활용하는 패턴입니다.

• 해외 여행을 가다
travel overseas = travel abroad = travel to foreign countries

• 가볼 만한 곳
great places to visit = wonderful places to visit = fantastic destinations

A I enjoy traveling abroad, but I'm also aware that Korea has many wonderful places to visit.
B That's so true. Going overseas is not always the best option. Every country has a lot of beautiful destinations of its own.

A 저는 해외 여행을 좋아하지만, 한국에도 가볼 만한 좋은 곳이 많다는 걸 알고 있습니다.
B 정말 그래요. 해외로 가는 게 항상 최선의 선택은 아닙니다. 나라마다 아름다운 여행지가 많죠.

쇼핑

95 온라인으로 물건 사는 걸 좋아합니다.

> I love shopping online.
> I love online shopping more than visiting a store.
> Online shopping is my favorite.

online은 형용사, 부사로 모두 쓰이죠. 첫번째 문장처럼 문장 끝에 두어 '온라인으로'라는 뜻으로 활용해도 되고, online shopping처럼 형용사로 활용해도 좋습니다.

> • 온라인 쇼핑을 좋아하다
> love shopping online = love online shopping = online shopping is my favorite

A I love online shopping more than visiting a store.
B Same here. It's just so convenient. I can find exactly what I need without the hassle.
A Exactly. No long lines or crowded stores to deal with.

A 저는 매장에 가는 것보다 온라인 쇼핑을 더 좋아해요.
B 저도요. 정말 편리하거든요. 번거로움 없이 필요한 걸 정확히 찾을 수 있어요.
A 맞아요. 긴 대기줄이나 붐비는 매장을 신경 쓰지 않아도 되죠.

96 옷이나 패션 소품들은 오프라인에서 사는 걸 더 좋아합니다.

As for clothes and other fashion items, I prefer shopping at offline stores.

For clothing and things I wear, I prefer going to real stores.

I prefer offline shopping for clothing and fashion.

온라인과 반대되는 오프라인 상점은 offline을 활용해 표현해도 좋고, 두번째 문장처럼 real store 혹은 physical store(물리적인 상점)라고 할 수도 있습니다.

> • 오프라인 쇼핑
> shopping at offline stores = going to real stores = offline shopping

A Do you shop online a lot?
B Not really. For clothing and things I wear, I prefer going to real stores.
A Me too. I like to try things on and see how they fit before buying.

A 온라인 쇼핑 많이 하시나요?
B 별로요. 옷이나 몸에 걸치는 물건은 실제 매장에서 사는 걸 선호해요.
A 저도요. 사기 전에 입어보고 잘 맞는지 확인하는 걸 좋아해요.

쇼핑

97 오프라인 상점에서는 거의 안 사는 것 같아요.

I almost never visit any brick-and-mortar stores anymore.

I buy almost everything online these days.

I don't really shop at physical stores anymore.

오프라인 상점을 가리키는 다른 표현에 brick-and-mortar store도 있습니다. brick은 벽돌을 말하고 mortar는 벽돌을 쌓을 때 쓰는 모르타르를 가리키죠. 즉 '건물'에서 유래하여 '오프라인'을 일컫게 되었습니다.

> • 오프라인 상점
> **brick-and-mortar stores = physical stores**

A I don't really shop at physical stores anymore.
B I also find online shopping so much more convenient. Plus, I can avoid the crowds and long lines.
A Exactly. It's a real time-saver.

A 저는 더 이상 오프라인 매장에서 안 사요.
B 저도 온라인 쇼핑이 훨씬 편리하다고 생각해요. 붐비지도 않고, 줄을 안 서도 되고요.
A 맞아요. 정말 시간을 절약할 수 있어요.

98 골목상권을 응원합니다.

I try to support my local mom-and-pop stores.

I prefer to support local business owners.

I always support my neighborhood shops.

가족이 운영하는 소규모 상점을 mom-and-pop store라고 하죠. 우리말 '골목상권'에 잘 어울리는 표현입니다.

> **• 골목상권**
> local mom-and-pop stores = local business owners = neighborhood shops

A Do you do most of your shopping online or in stores?
B I try to support my local mom-and-pop stores.
A That's great! Why do you prefer local stores?
B I love the personal touch I can feel at the neighborhood stores.

A 쇼핑을 온라인으로 하나요 매장을 직접 가나요?
B 저는 동네 상점을 도우려고 노력합니다.
A 좋네요! 왜 골목 상권을 선호하시나요?
B 동네 매장에서 느낄 수 있는 친근감을 좋아합니다.

쇼핑

99 새 플레이스테이션에 눈독들이고 있어요. 세일하면 살 겁니다.

I have my eye set on a new PlayStation. I'm going to get one when it's on sale.

I'm eyeing a new PlayStation. I'll wait until the price drops, though.

I'm considering picking up a new PlayStation. I'll get one when it's a little cheaper.

우리말 속어 '찜해 두다'에 해당하는 영어 표현이 have my eye set on something 이죠. 두번째 문장처럼 eye를 동사로 쓰면, 그냥 보는 것이 아니라, 의심의 눈초리를 보내거나 갖고 싶어 쳐다본다는 뜻입니다.

- 눈독들이고 있다
have my eye set on = be eyeing = consider picking up

- 세일하면
when it's on sale = when the price drops = when it's a little cheaper

A I have my eye set on a new PlayStation. I'm going to get it when it's on sale.
B Nice! I heard the new PlayStation has some amazing features.

A 새 플레이스테이션을 눈여겨보고 있어요. 세일 때 사야겠어요.
B 좋네요! 새 버전에 놀라운 기능들이 있다고 들었어요.

100 해외 직구를 좋아합니다.

I love shopping from overseas shopping sites.

I love using international shopping sites.

I prefer international online marketplaces.

'직구'를 한 단어로 표현하기는 어렵고, 해외 쇼핑 사이트에서 구입한다고 표현하면 적당하죠. 온라인 장터를 뜻하는 외래어 '오픈 마켓'을 영어로 open market이라고 하면 어색합니다. online marketplace가 맞는 표현입니다.

> • 해외직구
> shopping from overseas shopping sites = using international shopping sites = using international online marketplaces

A I love shopping from overseas shopping sites such as Amazon or Rakuten.
B Really? What do you usually buy from there?
A Mostly unique items that I can't find locally, like specific gadgets and fashion brands. The variety is amazing.

A 아마존이나 라쿠텐 같은 해외 사이트에서 쇼핑하는 걸 좋아해요.
B 정말요? 보통 뭐 사세요?
A 주로 한국에 없는 독특한 아이템들이요. 특정 기기나 패션 브랜드 같은 거죠. 정말 다양해요.

쇼핑

101 관세를 내고도 해외에서 사는 것이 더 저렴해요.

> Even after paying tariffs, buying from overseas shopping sites is cheaper.
>
> Even after taxes, it's cheaper to use foreign shopping sites.
>
> Even with import fees, I save a lot of money purchasing through overseas online marketplaces.

'관세'는 영어로 tariff이죠. 두번째 문장처럼 세금(tax)이라고 하거나, 세번째 문장처럼 수입비용(import fee)이라고 해도 의미가 잘 통합니다.

> • 관세를 내고도
> even after paying taxes/tariffs = even after taxes = even with import fees

A Have you ever tried buying things from overseas shopping sites?
B Absolutely. Even after paying tariffs, buying from overseas shopping sites is cheaper.
A Really? That's surprising. I always thought the extra charges would make it more expensive.

A 해외 쇼핑 사이트에서 물건 사 본 적 있어요?
B 물론이죠. 관세를 내도 해외에서 직구하는 게 더 저렴해요.
A 정말요? 놀랍네요. 저는 추가 비용 때문에 더 비쌀 거라고 생각했어요.

102 항상 가격 비교 사이트를 보고 최저가로 삽니다.

> Whatever I buy, I visit price comparison sites and choose the best price.
>
> Whatever I purchase, I use a price comparison site to find the best deal.
>
> No matter what I buy, I compare prices on a site and pick the best one.

'가격 비교 사이트'는 우리말을 그대로 옮겨 price comparison site라고 하면 됩니다. 두번째 문장의 best deal은 싸고 좋은 상품을 구입하는 것을 말하죠.

> • 최저가로 사다
> choose the best price = find the best deal = pick the best one

A Do you shop online often?
B Absolutely. Whatever I purchase, I use a price comparison site to find the best deal.
A I should start doing that too. It will save me a lot of money.

A 온라인 쇼핑 자주 하시나요?
B 물론이죠. 무엇을 사든 가격 비교 사이트를 이용해서 최저가를 찾습니다.
A 저도 그렇게 해야겠어요. 돈을 많이 아낄 수 있겠네요.

반려동물

103 반려동물 있으세요? 저는 고양이를 키워요.

> Do you have pets? I have a cat.
>
> Any pets? I have a cat at home.
>
> Do you have pets? I've got just one cat.

우리는 '애완동물'보다 '반려동물'이라는 표현을 더 바람직하게 느끼지만, 영어로는 companion animal 대신 pet이 일상에서 여전히 많이 쓰이고 있습니다.

> **• 고양이를 키운다**
> have a cat = have a cat at home = have got just one cat

A Do you have pets? I have a cat.
B Yes, I have a dog. What's your cat's name?
A Her name is Luna. What about your dog?

A 반려동물이 있나요? 저는 고양이를 키워요.
B 네, 저는 개를 키우고 있어요. 고양이 이름은 뭐예요?
A 루나예요. 멍멍이 이름은요?

104 멍멍이한테 손이 많이 가지만, 제게는 가족이나 마찬가지입니다.

> I need to take a lot of care of my dog, but he is like family to me.
>
> My dog needs a lot of care, but he's basically my family.
>
> Dogs are a lot of work, but I don't mind because he's like family to me.

'손이 많이 간다'는 많은 도움을 필요로 한다는 의미이므로, take/need a lot of care로 표현할 수 있습니다. 세번째 문장처럼 '많은 일거리(work)이다'라고 해도 같은 뜻이죠.

> **• 멍멍이한테 손이 많이 간다**
> take a lot of care of my dog = my dog needs a lot of care = dogs are a lot of work

A I need to take a lot of care of my dog, but he is like family to me.
B I totally understand. Pets bring so much joy, don't they?
A Absolutely. What about you? Do you have any pets?

A 멍멍이한테 손이 많이 가지만, 제게는 가족이나 마찬가지입니다.
B 완전 이해해요. 반려동물은 정말 우리를 기쁘게 해주잖아요.
A 물론이죠. 어떠세요? 반려동물이 있으신가요?

반려동물

105 한국에서도 반려동물에 관한 문화가 많이 발전하고 시장도 커지고 있습니다.

> The culture about pets has become more sophisticated in Korea, and the market is getting bigger.
>
> The pet culture in Korea continues to advance, and the market grows ever larger.
>
> Pet culture is becoming more developed in Korea, and so is the market opportunity.

문화가 발전하는 것은 더 세련되어진다는 의미에서 sophisticated라고 해도 좋고, 발전한다는 뜻을 지닌 advance, develop과 같은 동사를 써도 좋습니다.

> **· 발전하다**
> become more sophisticated = continue to advance = become more developed

A The culture about pets has become more sophisticated in Korea, and the market is getting bigger.

B Yeah, it's amazing how much it's changed over the years. There are so many pet cafes and boutiques now.

A 한국에서도 반려동물 문화가 많이 발전하고 시장도 커지고 있습니다.

B 네, 몇 년간 놀라울 정도로 많이 바뀌었죠. 지금은 반려동물 카페와 부티크가 정말 많아요.

106 사람에게 더 친근하게 굴어서 고양이보다 개를 더 좋아합니다.

I love dogs better than cats as dogs feel closer to people than cats.

I prefer dogs over cats because I feel like dogs are more similar to people.

I'm more of a dog person than a cat person because dogs are pure souls.

개를 좋아하는 사람을 dog person, 고양이를 좋아하는 사람은 cat person이라고 합니다. 두번째와 세번째 문장의 Dogs are similar to people. Dogs are pure souls.는 모두 사람에게 친근한 개의 특성을 칭찬하는 표현들입니다.

> • 사람에게 더 친근하다
> feel closer to people = be more similar to people = be pure souls

A I love dogs better than cats as dogs feel closer to people than cats.
B I get that. Dogs are definitely more affectionate and loyal.
A Yeah, they always seem so happy to see you, no matter what.

A 사람에게 더 친근하게 굴어서 고양이보다 개를 더 좋아합니다.
B 이해가 가요. 개는 확실히 더 애정이 많고 충성스럽죠.
A 네. 어떤 상황에서든 주인을 보면 기뻐하는 듯하잖아요.

반려동물

107 털이 덜 빠져서 고양이보다 개를 더 좋아합니다.

> I love dogs better than cats as dogs' hair fall out less than cats.
>
> I love dogs more than cats because some dogs shed less.
>
> I prefer dogs to cats because some dogs don't lose so much fur.

'털이 빠지다'는 fall out이라고 표현할 수 있는데, 한 단어로 shed라고 해도 좋습니다. 세번째 문장처럼 lose fur라고 할 수도 있죠. 동물의 긴 털을 fur라고 합니다.

> • 털이 덜 빠진다
> hair fall out less = shed less = not lose so much fur

A I love dogs better than cats as dogs' hair falls out less than cats.
B That's true. Dog fur can be easier to manage.
A Plus, dogs are so friendly and loyal.

A 고양이보다 개를 더 좋아해요. 개는 고양이보다 털이 덜 빠지거든요.
B 맞아요. 개 털이 관리하기 더 쉬울 수 있죠.
A 게다가 개는 너무 다정하고 충성스러워요.

108 더 깔끔하고 독립적이라서 개보다 고양이를 좋아합니다.

> I love cats better than dogs as cats have better cleanliness and more independence.
>
> I love cats more than dogs because cats are cleaner and more independent.
>
> I'm more of a cat person than a dog person because cats are very clean and not so needy.

clean에서 파생된 cleanliness는 [클렌리니스]로 발음합니다. 발음에 주의할 단어죠. 세번째 문장의 needy는 도움을 필요로 한다는 뜻인데, 손길이 많이 가는 반려동물의 특성을 표현하기에도 적당한 단어입니다.

> **· (특성이) 더 깔끔하다**
> have better cleanliness = be cleaner = be very clean

A I love cats better than dogs as cats have better cleanliness and more independence.
B That makes sense. Cats are pretty low-maintenance compared to dogs.
A Exactly! They're so easy to take care of, and I appreciate how they can entertain themselves.

A 더 깔끔하고 독립적이라서 개보다 고양이를 더 좋아합니다.
B 그럴 수도 있겠네요. 고양이는 개에 비하면 관리를 덜 해줘도 되죠.
A 맞아요! 고양이는 돌보기 쉽고, 혼자 잘 놀아 줘서 고맙죠.

반려동물

109 신경을 덜 써줘도 돼서 개보다 고양이를 더 좋아합니다.

> I love cats better than dogs as cats need less attention than dogs.
>
> I love cats more than dogs because cats aren't so needy.
>
> I prefer cats to dogs since cats don't need so much attention.

'주의'나 '주목'을 뜻하는 attention을 덜 필요로 한다고 말하면 신경을 덜 써도 된다는 뜻이 되죠.

> • 신경을 덜 써줘도 된다
> need less attention = not so needy = not need so much attention

A I love cats better than dogs as cats need less attention than dogs.
B That's true. Cats are pretty independent and can take care of themselves.
A Exactly! I appreciate that they don't require constant attention.

A 신경을 덜 써줘도 돼서 개보다 고양이를 더 좋아합니다.
B 맞아요. 고양이는 상당히 독립적이어서 스스로를 돌볼 수 있죠.
A 맞습니다! 고양이는 계속 관심을 가져주지 않아도 되니 고맙죠.

110 개나 고양이 말고, 좀 특별한 반려동물을 키워 보고 싶습니다.

> I'm interested in keeping a unique pet instead of a dog or cat.
>
> I want to raise a special pet other than a dog or cat.
>
> I would love to own an uncommon pet rather than the usual dog or cat.

반려동물을 키운다고 할 때 쓰는 동사는 keep, raise가 일반적입니다. 소유한다는 뜻인 own도 있죠. 반면, grow는 식물을 키우는 경우에만 활용하고, 반려동물을 키운다고 할 때는 쓰지 않습니다.

> • 반려동물을 키우다
> keep a pet = raise a pet = own a pet

A I want to raise a special pet other than a dog or cat.
B Someone I know keeps a lizard and says it's much cuter and friendlier than you might think.

A 개나 고양이 말고, 좀 특별한 반려동물을 키워 보고 싶습니다. .
B 제가 아는 사람은 도마뱀을 키우는데, 키워보면 생각보다 귀엽고 친근감이 느껴진대요.

Exercise 2 다음 중 의미가 다른 문장 하나를 고르세요.

01
어떤 취미가 있으세요?

① So, what do you do for fun?
② So, any hobbies?
③ What line of work are you in?
④ What do you like to do for fun?

02
저한테는 안 맞더라고요.

① It wasn't my pain in the neck.
② It wasn't my cup of tea.
③ It didn't really suit me.
④ It wasn't really my thing.

03
돈이 문제가 안 된다면 어떤 취미를 가져보고 싶은가요?

① If money were no object, what hobby would you have?
② If you didn't have to worry about money, what would you do for a hobby?
③ If you were super-rich, what hobby would you pick up?
④ If the budget were limited, what would be your best choice for fun?

04
느끼한 음식 좋아합니다.

① My favorites are light foods.
② I love foods that are cheesy.
③ All my favorite foods are fatty.
④ I really love oily foods.

05
진짜 그 지역의 특색을 느낄 수 있는 덜 알려진 곳을 방문하고 싶어요.

① I'd love to visit relatively unknown areas where I can really feel the characteristics of the region.
② I'd love to get off the beaten path and enjoy some authentic local culture.
③ I'd rather poke around and see how the locals live.
④ I don't want to leave the well-trodden path when I'm visiting a foreign country.

06

오프라인 쇼핑을 더 좋아합니다.

① I prefer buying at brick-and-mortar stores.
② I prefer shopping at offline stores.
③ I prefer going to real stores.
④ I prefer digital purchasing for its convenience.

07

골목상권을 응원합니다.

① I try to support my local mom-and-pop stores.
② I love using mass retailers.
③ I prefer to support local business owners.
④ I always support my neighborhood shops.

08

개가 고양이보다 사람에게 더 친근하게 느껴집니다.

① Dogs are less social with people.
② Dogs feel closer to people than cats.
③ I feel like dogs are more similar to people.
④ Dogs are pure souls.

09

개가 고양이보다 털이 덜 빠집니다.

① Some dogs blow their coat more than cats.
② Dogs' hair fall out less than cats.
③ Some dogs shed less than cats.
④ Some dogs don't lose so much fur as cats

Exercise 2   정답 및 해설

01
3번 문장의 line of work는 어떤 직업군에 속해 있는지를 물을 때 쓰는 표현입니다. 취미가 아니라 '직종'을 묻는 표현이므로 의미가 다릅니다.

02
1번의 pain in the neck은 '골칫거리'라는 뜻입니다. 내게 어울리는 것을 말하는 나머지 세 문장과 의미가 다릅니다.

03
'돈'을 '예산'을 뜻하는 budget으로 표현하는 경우가 많습니다. 4번 문장은 '예산이 제한되어 있다면 어떤 선택이 최선이겠냐'는 뜻이므로 의미가 다르죠.

04
1번의 light foods는 말 그대로 '가벼운 음식'을 말합니다.

05
4번의 well-trodden path 역시 2번의 beaten path 처럼 많은 사람이 다녀서 '다져진 길'을 일컫습니다. well-trodden path에서 벗어나고 싶지 않다고 했으므로 낯선 곳은 가고 싶지 않다는 말이 되죠. 답은 4번입니다.

06
1번의 brick-and-mortar는 벽을 쌓을 때 쓰는 벽돌(brick)과 모르타르(mortar)를 일컫는 표현으로, 오프라인 상의 건물을 가리킵니다. 4번의 digital purchasing은 결국 온라인 상의 구매를 가리키므로 나머지 문장과 의미가 다르죠.

07
2번의 mass retailer는 '대규모 유통사'를 뜻하므로, '골목상권'과는 의미가 다릅니다.

08
1번의 social은 사교성이 있고 잘 어울리는 모습을 가리키죠. less social이라고 했으므로 사람에게 친근하지 않다는 뜻이 됩니다.

09
1번의 blow one's coat는 털갈이를 한다는 뜻입니다. '고양이보다 털갈이를 더 많이 하는 개도 있다'라는 뜻이므로 나머지 문장들과 의미가 다릅니다.

정답 1.③ 2.① 3.④ 4.① 5.④ 6.④ 7.② 8.① 9.①

문화, 스포츠를 말하는 스몰토크

스포츠
드라마
음악
영화
Exercise 3

스포츠

111 어릴 때부터 드래곤즈의 왕팬입니다.

> I've been a huge fan of the Dragons since I was a child.
> I'm a lifelong fan of the Dragons.
> I've supported the Dragons my whole life.

평생 그랬다는 말은 since I was a child(어릴 때부터)라고 해도 되고, 말 그대로 '평생'을 표현하는 lifelong 혹은 my whole life와 같은 표현을 활용해도 좋죠.

> • 어릴 때부터 (드래곤즈) 팬이다
> a huge fan since I was a child = a lifelong fan = supported the Dragons my whole life

A I'm a lifelong fan of the Dragons.
B That's awesome! How long have you been supporting them?
A Ever since I can remember. I grew up watching their games with my family.

A 저는 평생 드래곤즈 팬이에요.
B 멋지네요! 얼마나 오랫동안 응원해 왔나요?
A 제가 기억하는 가장 어릴 때부터요. 가족과 함께 드래곤즈 경기를 보며 자랐습니다.

112 어떤 팀을 응원하나요?

> Who do you cheer for?
>
> Who's your team?
>
> Which team do you rep?

팀을 응원하는 것은 cheer for 혹은 root for라고 합니다. 세번째 문장의 rep은 represent의 준말인데, 대표한다는 기본 뜻에서 나아가, 스포츠 팀을 응원하고 지지를 보낸다는 의미로 쓰입니다.

> • 팀을 응원하다
> cheer for = your team = rep

A Do you follow any sports?
B Yes, I'm really into football. I'm a fan of Dragons. Who's your team?
A I'm a huge fan of Knights. They've been my favorite since I was a kid.

A 관심 갖는 스포츠 있으세요?
B 네, 저는 축구를 정말 좋아해요. 드래곤즈 팬입니다. 어떤 팀 응원하세요?
A 저는 나이츠의 열렬한 팬이에요. 어렸을 때부터 제가 가장 좋아했던 팀이죠.

스포츠

113 그 선수 지난 시즌에는 별로였지만 이번 시즌에는 잘 하기를 바라요.

> The player didn't do a very good job last season, but I expect he'll do better this year.
>
> The player wasn't great last season, but I have high hopes for him this season.
>
> The player wasn't up to snuff last season, but I think he'll play better this time around.

뭔가를 잘한다고 할 때 쓰는 가장 흔한 표현들을 소개하고 있습니다. 세번째 문장의 up to snuff는 기준에 달하거나 기대에 부합한다는 뜻의 속어 표현이죠. not과 함께 기대에 못 미친다는 뜻으로 쓰였습니다.

> **• (선수의 성적이) 별로였다**
> didn't do a very good job = wasn't great last season = wasn't up to snuff

A The player didn't do so well last season, but I expect he'll do better this year.
B That's what I want, too. I've heard he's been putting in a lot of extra practice.
A That's good to hear. I hope all that hard work pays off.

A 그 선수, 지난 시즌에는 잘하지 못했지만, 올해는 나아질 것으로 기대해요.
B 저도 그래요. 연습을 많이 하고 있다고 들었어요.
A 좋은 소식이네요. 열심히 노력한 게 결실을 맺기를 바랍니다.

114 그 선수 능력도 출중하지만 개인 생활도 깨끗해서 좋아합니다.

> He is great on the field, but his private life is so clean. That's why I like him better.
>
> He's a great player, but his private life is scandal-free. That's why I like him best.
>
> He's an inspiration on and off the field. That's why I like him best.

경기장에서의 모습은 on the field, 경기장 밖에서의 모습은 off the field로 표현할 수 있습니다. '사생활이 깨끗하다'는 말 그대로 clean이라고 해도 좋고, 스캔들이 없다는 의미로 scandal-free처럼 말할 수도 있습니다.

> **• 개인 생활도 깨끗하다**
> private life is so clean = private life is scandal-free = be an inspiration on and off the field

A Who is your favorite player on the team?
B David Parker. He's a great player, but his private life is scandal-free. That's why I like him best.
A I totally get that. I also love those who stays out of trouble off the field.

A 팀에서 가장 좋아하는 선수는 누구예요?
B 데이비드 파커요. 선수로서 훌륭한데, 사생활에서도 스캔들이 없어요. 그래서 그를 가장 좋아합니다.
A 이해가 가요. 저도 경기장 밖에서도 문제가 없는 선수를 좋아합니다.

스포츠

115 유럽 축구를 즐겨 봅니다. 한국 선수들도 있잖아요.

> I love watching European soccer league. There are Korean players there, too.
>
> I'm a big fan of European soccer league, which also feature Korean players.
>
> I love following a soccer league in Europe, and it's great to see Korean players there too.

스포츠 등 어떤 분야에 관심이 있는 모습을 동사 follow만으로 표현할 수 있습니다. 세번째 문장에서 활용하고 있죠. 두번째 문장의 feature는 특징으로 포함하고 있거나 특징이 된다는 의미인데, 일대일로 대응하는 우리말이 없지만 영어에서는 빈번히 활용되는 동사입니다.

• ~를 즐겨 보다
love watching ~ = be a big fan of ~ = love following ~

• 한국 선수들도 있다
there are Korean players = the league also features Korean players = see Korean players there

---

A Do you watch a lot of soccer?
B Yes. I really enjoy the Premier League. There are Korean players, too.
A I agree. It's great to see Korean players making a name for themselves there.

A 축구 많이 보시나요?
B 예. 프리미어리그를 정말 좋아해요. 한국 선수들도 있잖아요.
A 맞아요. 한국 선수들이 프리미어리그에서 유명해지는 걸 보면 좋죠.

116 유럽이나 미국에서 뛰는 한국 야구 축구 선수들 보면 자랑스러워요.

> I feel proud when I see those Korean baseball or soccer players playing in Europe or North America.
>
> Seeing Korean baseball or soccer players compete in Europe or North America makes me proud.
>
> I take pride in seeing Korean athletes perform in European or North American baseball and soccer leagues.

'자랑스럽게 생각하다'는 be proud of, take pride in으로 표현할 수 있습니다. 두번째 문장은 '선수들을 보는 것이 나를 자랑스럽게 만든다'라는 영어식 문장 구조로 되어 있죠.

> • 자랑스럽다
> feel proud = make me proud = take pride in

A I feel proud when I see those Korean baseball or soccer players playing in Europe or North America.
B Yeah, it's great to see athletes representing their country on such a big stage.
A 우리나라 야구 선수, 축구 선수들이 유럽이나 북미에서 뛰는 걸 보면 자랑스러워요.
B 맞아요. 큰 무대에서 자기 나라를 대표하는 선수들을 보는 건 좋은 일이죠.

드라마

117 그 드라마 스토리가 뻔한데 계속 보게 됩니다.

The storyline is very conventional, but I keep watching the drama.

The storyline is very cookie-cutter, but I keep watching the show anyways.

The storyline is nothing special, but I can't stop watching.

conventional은 특별함 없이 뻔한 것을 가리키는 형용사입니다. cookie-cutter는 쿠키를 만드는 틀로 찍어낸 듯하다는 의미로, 우리말 '붕어빵처럼'에 해당하는 표현입니다.

> • 뻔하다
> conventional = cookie-cutter = nothing special

A Have you been watching anything interesting lately?
B Yes, I started this new series. The storyline is very cookie-cutter, but I keep watching the show anyways.
A What keeps you coming back to it?
B I think it's the characters. They're really captivating and well-acted.

A 요즘 보는 재밌는 프로그램 있습니까?
B 예, 새로운 시리즈를 보기 시작했어요. 스토리 라인은 뻔한데, 어쨌든 계속 봅니다.
A 어떤 점 때문에 계속 보게 되나요?
B 캐릭터 때문인 것 같아요. 매력이 있고 연기를 잘합니다.

118 그 드라마는 현실을 적나라하게 묘사하는 것 같아요.

I think the drama describes our real life very vividly.

I think that show precisely describes our real life.

It's like the drama holds a mirror up to our lives.

생생하다는 의미를 표현할 때 가장 먼저 떠올릴 단어는 vivid(ly)입니다. 두번째 문장의 precisely는 정교하다는 뜻이죠. 세번째 문장의 hold a mirror up to ~는 말 그대로 '~에 거울을 갖다 댄다', 즉 거울에 비친 듯 있는 그대로 묘사한다는 뜻입니다.

> • 현실을 적나라하게 묘사하다
> describe our real life very vividly = precisely describe our real life = hold a mirror up to our lives

A Have you been watching any new dramas lately?
B Yes, I started watching a new one recently. I think the drama describes our real life very vividly.
A That sounds intriguing. What makes it feel so realistic?
B The characters go through everyday struggles and emotions that we all experience.

A 최근에 새로운 드라마 보는 것 있나요?
B 네, 최근에 새로운 드라마 보기 시작했어요. 우리 실제 삶을 아주 생생하게 묘사한다고 생각합니다.
A 흥미롭네요. 어떤 점 때문에 현실적으로 느껴지나요?
B 우리 모두 경험하는 일상적인 어려움과 감정을 등장인물들도 겪어요.

드라마

119 스토리가 참신하고 전개가 빨라요.

> The storyline is new, and the story unfolds fast.
>
> The storyline is something different, and it's very fast-paced.
>
> The plot is really unusual, and things happen one after another.

unfold는 fold, 즉 '접다'의 반대이므로, 이야기를 '펼치다', '전개하다'라는 뜻입니다. 세번째 문장의 one after another는 어떤 일에 뒤이어 다른 일이 일어나는 모습, 즉 연달아 발생하는 모습을 표현합니다.

> **• 스토리 전개가 빠르다**
> story unfolds fast = storyline is fast-paced = things happen one after another

A There's this show that I started watching last week. The storyline is new and the story unfolds fast.
B That sounds exciting. What genre is it?
A It's a mystery thriller. Every episode leaves me on the edge of my seat.

A 제가 지난주부터 보기 시작한 프로가 있습니다. 이야기가 새롭고 전개가 빨라요.
B 재미있을 것 같네요. 어떤 장르인가요?
A 미스터리 스릴러입니다. 매 회마다 긴장하게 만들어요.

120 한국 드라마는 배경이 어떻든 항상 연애 얘기만 하는 것 같아요.

Whatever the background is, Korean dramas always seem to deal with love stories.

The main characters of Korean dramas always fall in love with each other, whatever the settings are.

No matter what the background situation is, Korean dramas always feature a love story.

드라마의 배경이나 상황 설정은 background 혹은 setting이라고 할 수 있습니다. Whatever처럼 -ever가 붙은 단어로 시작하는 문장은 No matter로 시작하는 문장으로도 바꿀 수 있죠.

• 연애 얘기를 다룬다
deal with love stories = characters fall in love with each other
= feature a love story

A Whatever the background is, Korean dramas always seem to deal with love stories.
B That's so true. There's always a romantic twist, regardless of the genre.
A Exactly. It's like they can't resist adding a love story, even in action or thriller series.

A 배경이 어떻든 한국 드라마는 늘 사랑 이야기를 다루는 것 같아요.
B 정말 그래요. 장르에 관계없이 항상 연애에 관한 반전이 있죠.
A 맞아요. 액션이나 스릴러 드라마에서도 사랑 얘기를 안 넣으면 안 되나봐요.

드라마

121 이 드라마, 아이들과 같이 보기에는 민망한 장면들이 있어요.

> Some of the scenes of the show are not appropriate to watch together with children.
>
> This show is inappropriate for kids.
>
> This is not a family-friendly show.

부정적인 내용일수록 세세히 말하기보다 적절히 돌려 표현하는 것이 바람직하죠. 이 때, 부적절하다는 의미를 지닌 inappropriate, not appropriate이 유용하죠. friendly는 친화적이라는 의미로, 다양한 단어와 함께 어울릴 수 있습니다. family-friendly이므로 가족들이 함께 하기에도 적합하다는 뜻이죠.

> • 아이들과 보기에 민망하다
> not appropriate to watch together with children =
> inappropriate for kids = not a family-friendly show

A Some of the scenes of the show are not appropriate to watch together with children.
B I didn't know that.
A You have to be careful with your children. It has some mature themes and scenes that wouldn't be suitable for kids.

A 그 프로의 일부 장면은 아이들과 함께 보기에 적합하지 않아요.
B 전 몰랐어요.
A 자녀와 함께 본다면 조심해야 합니다. 아이들에게 적합하지 않은 성인용 주제와 장면이 있어요.

122 잘생긴 남녀가 많이 나오는 프로그램을 좋아해요.

> I love shows that feature a lot of good-looking men and women.
>
> I love shows that include attractive actors and actresses.
>
> I mainly watch shows that showcase hot characters.

잘생기거나 예쁘다는 뜻으로 일반적인 단어가 good-looking입니다. 세번째처럼 hot이라는 구어적 표현을 쓸 수도 있죠. 세번째 문장의 showcase는 '진열장'인데, 동사로 '보여주다'라는 뜻도 지닙니다.

• 잘생긴 남녀(배우)
good-looking men and women = attractive actors and actresses = hot characters

A Have you been watching any new shows lately?
B Yes, I've been hooked on this new series. I love shows that feature a lot of good-looking men and women.
A That's always a plus. Which show are you talking about?

A 최근에 새로운 프로그램 시청하는 것 있나요?
B 네, 새로운 시리즈에 푹 빠졌어요. 저는 잘생긴 남녀가 많이 나오는 프로를 좋아하거든요.
A 잘생긴 사람들이 나오면 좋죠. 어떤 프로를 말씀하시는 건가요?

음악

123. 고등학교 친구들과 밴드를 하고 있어요. 저는 드럼을 칩니다.

> I have a band with my high school friends. I play the drums.
>
> I'm in a band with my high school buddies. I play the drums.
>
> I'm a drummer for my band that I have with my high school friends.

'드럼을 친다'는 play the drums도 좋고 명사 drummer를 활용해도 되죠. 밴드를 결성하는 것은 form a band라고 하고, 밴드의 일원이라면 have a band, be in a band처럼 표현하면 됩니다.

- 밴드를 하고 있다
have a band = be in a band

A Do you play any musical instruments?
B I have a band with my high school friends. I play the drums.
A That's so cool. What kind of music do you guys play?
B We mostly play rock and a bit of alternative.

A 연주하는 악기 있으세요?
B 고등학교 친구들과 밴드를 하고 있어요. 저는 드럼을 칩니다.
A 멋지네요. 어떤 음악을 연주하나요?
B 주로 록이고 얼터너티브도 약간 합니다.

124 악기를 배우고 싶은데, 시간이 잘 안 납니다.

> I'd love to learn how to play a musical instrument, but I don't have time to spare.
>
> I'd love to learn to play something, but I just don't have free time.
>
> I really want to learn how to play an instrument, but these days, my schedule is already packed.

spare를 time과 함께 쓰면 시간을 할애한다는 뜻이 됩니다. 세번째 문장의 packed는 무엇으로 가득 차 있다는 의미죠. 스케줄이 꽉 차 있다는 뜻으로 My schedule is packed.라고 표현했습니다.

> **• 시간이 안 난다**
> not have time to spare = not have free time = my schedule is already packed

A Do you play any musical instruments?
B I'd love to learn to play something, but I just don't have free time.
A I understand. There are so many things to juggle.

A 연주하는 악기 있으세요?
B 악기를 배우고 싶은데 여유 시간이 없네요.
A 이해합니다. 신경 써야 할 일들이 너무 많죠.

음악

콘서트 가는 것 좋아합니다. 라이브 공연을 보면 다르거든요.

> I love going to concerts. When you listen to the live performance, it's so different.
>
> I enjoy attending concerts because listening to a live performance is such a unique experience.
>
> I love the thrill of attending concerts. Live music feels so much more special.

콘서트에 가는 것은 go to a concert, attend a concert처럼 표현할 수 있습니다. attend는 회의나 수업에 참석하는 것뿐 아니라 행사나 공연에 가는 것을 일컫기도 하죠.

> • 콘서트에 가다
> go to concerts = attend concerts

A Have you been to any concerts lately?
B Yes, I went to one last weekend. I love the thrill of attending concerts. Live music feels so much more special.
A I totally agree. There's just something about the energy of a live performance.

A 최근에 가본 콘서트 있나요?
B 네, 지난 주말에 갔습니다. 콘서트에 가서 느끼는 스릴을 좋아해요. 라이브 음악은 훨씬 더 특별하게 느껴지잖아요.
A 전적으로 동의해요. 라이브 공연의 에너지는 뭔가 특별하죠.

126 록 음악 좋아합니다. 에너지와 강한 비트가 좋아요.

> I love rock music. I like the energy and the strong beat of the music.
>
> Rock music is my personal favorite. I love the energy it has, and I love songs with a good beat.
>
> Rock music is the best! I like it for its energetic beat.

favorite은 형용사로 익숙하지만, 두번째 문장처럼 명사로 쓸 수도 있습니다. 에너지와 비트를 하나로 합쳐 세번째 문장에서처럼 energetic beat라고 해도 좋죠.

• 에너지와 강한 비트
energy and the strong beat = energy and a good beat = energetic beat

---

A What kind of music do you enjoy?
B I love rock music. I like the energy and the strong beat of the music.
A Rock music is amazing. Do you have a favorite band?
B I really enjoy bands in the 70s. Their music is timeless.

A 어떤 음악을 좋아하세요?
B 록 음악을 좋아해요. 록의 에너지와 강한 비트가 좋아요.
A 록 음악 좋죠. 좋아하는 밴드가 있나요?
B 70년대 밴드를 정말 좋아해요. 그들의 음악은 시대를 초월합니다.

음악

127 재즈 좋아합니다. 연주자들의 자유로움 때문에요. 재즈는 자유를 느끼게 해주는 음악 같습니다.

> I love jazz. I love the freedom the jazz players are enjoying. It feels like a type of music that gives me a sense of freedom.
>
> Jazz captivates me. When jazz players are jamming, I can feel the freedom. It makes me feel free, too!
>
> Jazz music is wonderful. I admire the liberty jazz musicians have in their performance. I can sense that at home, too.

자유는 freedom 혹은 liberty로 표현하면 됩니다. 두번째 문장의 jam은 대중음악가들이 함께 즉흥연주를 하는 것을 말하죠. '연주한다'는 뜻으로 활용했습니다.

- **재즈 음악을 좋아하다**
I love jazz = Jazz captivates me = Jazz music is wonderful

- **자유를 느끼게 해 주다**
give me a sense of freedom = make me feel free = I can sense the liberty

A What kind of music do you enjoy?
B I love jazz music. When jazz players are jamming, I can feel the freedom. It makes me feel free, too!
A Yeah, jazz has such a unique vibe and energy.

A 어떤 음악 좋아하세요?
B 저는 재즈를 좋아합니다. 즉흥 연주를 하는 재즈 연주자들을 보면 자유를 느낄 수 있어요. 저도 자유로움을 느끼게 해 주죠!
A 맞아요. 재즈에는 독특한 분위기와 에너지가 있죠.

클래식 음악 팬입니다. 클래식 연주자들의 섬세한 감정 표현을 좋아해요.

> I love classical music. I love the delicate expression of feelings and emotions by the classical music players.
>
> I admire the subtle way classical musicians convey their emotions and feelings.
>
> The gentle emotional expression of classical music performers resonates with me deeply.

'섬세하다'와 잘 어울리는 영어 단어는 delicate입니다. subtle은 '미묘한' 정도 의미인데, 작은 차이를 가리킵니다. 세번째 문장의 resonate는 울리거나 반향을 일으킨다는 뜻이죠. Something resonates with me.처럼 말하면 '내게 울림을 준다'라는 말입니다.

> • **섬세한 감정 표현**
> delicate expression of feelings and emotions = subtle way classical musicians convey their emotions = gentle emotional expression

A I love classical music. I love the delicate expression of emotions by the classical music players.
B That's beautiful. Classical music has a way of touching the soul.
A Absolutely. The compositions are so detailed, too.

A 저는 클래식 음악을 좋아합니다. 클래식 음악 연주자들의 섬세한 감정 표현이 좋아요.
B 멋지네요. 클래식 음악은 영혼의 울림을 불러일으키죠.
A 맞습니다. 작곡도 섬세하죠.

영화

129 잘생기고 연기도 잘 해서 김갑돌을 좋아합니다.

I like Kim very much. He is very good-looking and is good at acting.

I like Kim so much! He's really attractive and a great actor.

I like Kim the most. He's a good-looking guy and has got serious acting chops.

세번째 문장의 acting chop은 연기 능력이나 기술을 가리킵니다. chop은 원래 내리쳐서 자르는 동작을 나타내는데, 무술에서 손으로 내리치는 동작을 일컫기도 합니다. 더 나아가 음악이나 연기 분야에서의 기술, 능력 등을 가리키게 되었죠.

- 잘생기다
good-looking = attractive

- 연기를 잘 하다
good at acting = a great actor = got serious acting chops

A I recently watched a movie with Ethan Williams in it. I like him very much. He is very good-looking and is good at acting.
B I agree. He's very talented and always gives a great performance.

A 최근에 이선 윌리엄스가 출연한 영화를 봤습니다. 제가 정말 좋아해요. 잘생겼고 연기도 잘합니다.
B 동의해요. 재능이 뛰어나고 항상 연기가 훌륭하죠.

130 잘생긴 외모에 그의 연기력이 가려지는 것 같습니다.

I think his acting is overshadowed by his nice appearance.

Honestly, he's too good-looking. I can't focus on his acting.

His appearance is a drawback for me. It distracts attention from his role.

'빛을 바래게 하다'에 해당하는 동사가 overshadow입니다. 두드러진 다른 어떤 것 때문에 원래 가치가 평가받지 못하는 상황을 말할 때 적절한 단어죠. 세번째 문장의 drawback은 결점이라는 뜻이고, distract는 주의를 분산시킨다는 의미입니다.

> **• 잘생긴 외모에 (연기력이) 가려지다**
> be overshadowed by his nice appearance = can't focus on his acting = distracts attention from his role

A I watched a new film with Anthony Rivera in it. I think his acting is overshadowed by his nice appearance.
B I know what you mean. He's really handsome, but his talent deserves more recognition.
A Exactly. He's got great acting skills, but people focus more on his looks.

A 앤서니 리베라가 출연한 새 영화를 봤어요. 그의 연기가 멋진 외모에 가려진 것 같아요.
B 무슨 말인지 알겠어요. 정말 잘생겼지만, 그의 재능은 더 인정받을 만해요.
A 맞습니다. 연기력이 정말 훌륭한데, 사람들은 그의 외모에 더 집중해요.

영화

131 너무 바빠서 요즘 무슨 영화가 상영 중인지도 몰랐어요.

I've been so busy lately that I don't know what kind of movies are on these days.

I've been so crushed with work that I have no idea what's showing in the theaters.

My schedule is packed, so I have no idea what's playing these days.

영화가 상영된다고 할 때 쓰는 동사는 show, play입니다. 첫번째 문장처럼 on 이라고만 해도 상영이 되고 있는 상태를 가리키죠. 두번째 문장의 crush는 압도하거나 박살낸다는 뜻이므로, be crushed with work는 많은 일에 압도된다는 의미입니다.

> • 무슨 영화가 상영 중인지
> what kind of movies are on = what's showing = what's playing

A Have you seen any good movies recently?
B I've been so crushed with work that I have no idea what's showing in the theaters.
A I understand. Work can get really overwhelming. There's a new action movie that just came out. Why don't you give it a try?

A 최근에 본 영화 중에 괜찮은 거 있었나요?
B 일에 너무 쫓겨서 무슨 영화가 상영 중인지도 전혀 모르겠어요.
A 이해가 갑니다. 일에 치일 수 있죠. 새로 나온 액션 영화가 있어요. 한 번 보세요.

132 어떤 영화를 제일 좋아하세요?

What's your favorite movie genre?
What kind of movies do you like?
What's your preferred film genre?

genre는 [잔러]와 같이 발음하면 됩니다. [쟝르]라고 발음하지 않도록 주의하세요.

> • 제일 좋아하는 영화 장르
> favorite movie genre = kind of movies I like = preferred film genre

A Do you have a favorite genre of movie?
B Yeah, I love sci-fi. There's something about exploring the unknown that really excites me. What about you?
A I'm more into comedies. I love a good laugh after a long day.

A 어떤 영화 장르를 좋아하세요?
B 네, 저는 공상과학 영화를 좋아해요. 미지의 세계를 탐험하는 영화에는 우리를 즐겁게 하는 특별함이 있죠. 어떤 영화 좋아하세요?
A 저는 코미디 좋아해요. 힘든 하루를 보내고 한바탕 웃는 걸 좋아해요.

영화

133. 반전이 기발한 영화를 좋아합니다.

> I love movies that have such a great twist at the ending.
> I love movies with a twist ending.
> I really enjoy movies that catch you off guard at the end.

영화나 소설의 반전은 twist라고 합니다. 세번째 문장의 catch somebody off guard는 '누군가를 가드를 내리고 있는 상태에서 잡다', 즉 의외의 질문이나 행동으로 놀라게 만든다는 뜻입니다. 관객을 놀라게 하는 예상밖의 반전을 말할 때도 적절한 표현이죠.

> • 반전이 기발하다
> have such a great twist = with a twist ending = catch you off guard at the end

A I love movies that have such a great twist at the ending.
B Those are the best. They keep you guessing until the very last moment.
A Exactly. It's so satisfying when the story takes an unexpected turn.

A 결말에 멋진 반전이 있는 영화를 좋아해요.
B 그런 영화 최고죠. 마지막 순간까지 궁금하게 만들잖아요.
A 맞아요. 이야기가 예상치 못한 방향으로 전개될 때 정말 만족스럽죠.

134 공포영화나 너무 잔인한 영화는 좋아하지 않아요.

I don't like scary movies or movies that have many disturbing scenes.

I don't like scary or gory movies.

I really dislike movies that scare me or gross me out.

scary는 무서운 것을 가리키고, gory는 유혈이 낭자하거나 흉측한 모습을 묘사하는 단어입니다. 그런 모습들은 모두 disturbing이라고 뭉뚱그려 설명할 수 있는데, 불편하게 만들고 잔인하다는 뜻입니다. gross가 역겹다는 뜻이므로, 세번째 문장의 gross somebody out은 잔인한 장면으로 역겹게 만드는 것을 가리킵니다.

> • 잔인한 장면이 많은 영화
> movies that have many disturbing scenes = gory movies = movies that gross me out

A I don't like scary movies or movies that have many disturbing scenes.
B I understand. Some of those make you really uncomfortable.
A Exactly. I love comedies and romantic films.

A 저는 무서운 영화나 불편한 장면이 많은 영화는 좋아하지 않습니다.
B 이해해요. 그런 영화들은 정말 사람을 불편하게 만들잖아요.
A 맞아요. 저는 코미디와 로맨틱한 영화를 좋아합니다.

영화

135 즐겁고 기분이 좋아지게 하는 영화를 좋아합니다.

> I love movies that are positive and heart-warming.
> I love movies that are uplifting and make me feel good.
> I love movies that are cheerful and emotionally positive.

여기 나오는 형용사들은 모두 좋은 기분, 긍정적인 기분을 묘사하는 단어들입니다. 우리말과 일대일로 짝을 지어 기억하기보다는 비슷한 의미로 이해하고 번갈아가며 써 보는 것이 중요합니다.

> • 즐겁게 하는
> positive = uplifting = cheerful
>
> • 기분이 좋아지게 하는
> heart-warming = that make me feel good = emotionally positive

A I love movies that are positive and heart-warming.
B Those are the best. They always leave you with a good feeling.
A Yes. I love it when a movie can make me smile.

A 저는 긍정적이고 마음을 따뜻하게 하는 영화를 좋아합니다.
B 그런 영화가 최고예요. 항상 기분 좋게 해주잖아요.
A 네. 영화가 저를 웃게 할 때 정말 좋아요.

136 액션 영화나 SF 영화를 좋아합니다. 극장에서 그런 영화를 보면 스트레스가 풀려요.

> I love action-packed movies or Sci-Fi movies. When I watch those movies at the theater, I feel like my stress is relieved.
>
> I love movies with crazy action or great sci-fi. Watching such a movie in the theater is a big stress relief for me.
>
> I love big blockbuster action and sci-fi movies. When I'm in the theater, all my stress just disappears.

액션 장면이 많은 영화를 action-packed movie라고 하죠. 스트레스를 해소한다고 할 때 쓰는 동사는 relieve, reduce, release 등 다양합니다. stress relief는 스트레스를 해소시켜주는 것을 일컫죠.

> • 액션 영화
>
> action-packed movies = movies with crazy action = blockbuster action movies

A What kind of movies do you enjoy?
B I love action-packed movies or Sci-Fi movies. When I watch those movies at the theater, I feel like my stress is relieved.
A I also like those movies. They help me escape from reality for a while.

A 어떤 영화 좋아하세요?
B 저는 액션이 많은 영화나 SF 영화를 좋아해요. 그런 영화를 극장에서 보면 스트레스가 풀리는 기분이 들어요.
A 저도 그런 영화 좋아해요. 잠시 현실에서 벗어나게 해주거든요.

영화

 어려운 예술 영화보다는 쉽고 편하게 즐길 수 있는 영화가 좋아요.

> I don't like those difficult art movies. I enjoy easy movies that make me have fun.
>
> I don't really go for complicated art films. I like simpler movies that make me feel good.
>
> I don't care for art-house movies. I like movies that are easy to grasp and fun to watch.

예술 영화는 art movie 혹은 art-house movie라고 하죠. 세번째 문장의 grasp는 잡는다는 뜻인데, 손에 잡듯 이해한다는 말도 됩니다. 참고로, art movie와 대비되는 부담 없는 상업적 영화를 popcorn flicks라고 하죠. 극장에서 팝콘을 먹으면서 편히 보는 영화라는 뜻입니다.

- 예술 영화
art films = art-house movies

- 쉬운 영화
easy movies = simpler movies that make me feel good = movies that are easy to grasp

A I love watching movies, but I don't really go for complicated art films. I like simpler movies that make me feel good.
B I get that. I also want to relax and enjoy something light.

A 저는 영화 보는 걸 좋아하지만, 복잡한 예술 영화는 별로예요. 기분이 좋아지는 단순한 영화를 좋아해요.
B 그래요. 저도 긴장을 풀고 가벼운 영화를 즐기려고 해요.

138 할리우드 영화는 너무 상업적이에요. 저는 제3세계 영화에 관심이 많아요.

> Hollywood movies are too commercial. I'm so interested in the Third World movies.
>
> Hollywood movies are soulless. I'm much more interested in independent films from developing countries.
>
> Hollywood films are so formulaic. I prefer international films from developing nations.

'상업적'은 commercial이라고 하지만, 할리우드 영화를 부정적으로 묘사할 때 soulless(소울이 없는), 혹은 formulaic(정형화된)처럼 표현할 수도 있습니다.

- **상업적인**
commercial = soulless = formulaic

A Hollywood movies are soulless. I'm much more interested in independent films from developing countries.
B That's interesting. What do you like about independent films?
A They often have unique stories and genuine emotions that Hollywood movies don't have.

A 할리우드 영화에는 영혼이 없어요. 저는 개발도상국의 독립 영화에 훨씬 더 관심이 있습니다.
B 흥미롭네요. 독립 영화의 어떤 점이 마음에 드시나요?
A 할리우드 영화에는 없는 독특한 스토리와 리얼한 감정 표현이 있죠.

Exercise 3

다음 중 의미가 다른 문장 하나를 고르세요.

01

어떤 팀을 응원하나요?

① Who do you cheer for?
② Do you sabotage any team?
③ Who's your team?
④ Which team do you rep?

02

그 드라마 스토리가 뻔해요.

① The storyline is full of surprises.
② The storyline is very conventional.
③ The storyline is very cookie-cutter.
④ The storyline is nothing special.

03

그 드라마는 현실을 적나라하게 묘사하는 것 같아요.

① I think the drama describes our real life very vividly.
② I think that show precisely describes our real life.
③ That show barely reflects anything about our real life.
④ It's like the drama holds a mirror up to our lives.

04

재즈는 자유로운 음악 같아 좋습니다.

① I love the freedom the jazz players are enjoying.
② Jazz musicians often adhere to specific styles or conventions.
③ When jazz players are jamming, I can feel the freedom.
④ I admire the liberty jazz musicians have in their performance.

05

잘생긴 외모에 그의 연기력이 가려지는 것 같습니다.

① I think his acting is overshadowed by his nice appearance.
② Honestly, he's too good-looking. I can't focus on his acting.
③ His appearance is a drawback for me. It distracts attention from his role.
④ His handsome appearance enhances his impressive acting skills.

06

너무 바빠서 요즘 무슨 영화가 상영 중인지도 몰랐어요.

① I don't know what kind of movies are on these days.
② I'm not sure which movies are currently in production these days.
③ I have no idea what's showing in the theaters.
④ I have no idea what's playing these days.

07

반전이 기발한 영화를 좋아합니다.

① I love movies that have such a great twist at the ending.
② I love movies with a twist ending.
③ I really enjoy movies that catch you off guard at the end.
④ I appreciate films with natural, straightforward conclusions

08

공포영화나 너무 잔인한 영화는 좋아하지 않아요.

① I don't love films that are easy to follow.
② I don't like movies that have many disturbing scenes.
③ I don't like scary or gory movies.
④ I really dislike movies that gross me out.

09

할리우드 영화는 너무 상업적이에요.

① Hollywood films push the boundaries of creativity.
② Hollywood movies are too commercial.
③ Hollywood movies are soulless.
④ Hollywood films are so formulaic.

Exercise 3   정답 및 해설

01
2번 문장의 sabotage는 '사보타주'라는 외래어로도 잘 등장하는 단어입니다. 방해하거나 봉쇄한다는 뜻이므로, 응원한다는 뜻인 나머지 문장들과는 반대되는 말입니다.

02
1번의 full of surprises는 새롭고 놀라운 점들이 많다는 뜻이죠.

03
3번의 barely는 거의 ~하지 않는다는 뜻이므로, '현실을 거의 반영하지 않는다'라고 해석할 수 있습니다. 나머지 문장들과 의미가 다르죠.

04
2번의 convention은 '관습'이나 '판에 박힌 것'을 가리킵니다. adhere to는 어떤 태도를 고수한다는 뜻이므로, '관습적인 것을 고수하는 재즈 뮤지션이 있다'라고 해석할 수 있죠.

05
4번의 enhance는 증진시킨다는 뜻이므로, 그의 외모가 연기력을 더 돋보이게 한다는 말이 되죠.

06
2번의 in production은 '제작 중'이라는 뜻이죠. 나머지 세 문장은 모두 '상영 중'을 가리키므로 의미가 다릅니다.

07
4번의 straightforward는 직설적이라는 뜻이죠. 반전이 없이 곧바로 진행되다가 끝나는 영화를 말하므로 의미가 다릅니다.

08
1번의 easy to follow는 쉽게 따라가며 볼 수 있는 영화를 가리키죠. 다른 문장들과 의미가 다릅니다.

09
1번의 push the boundaries는 '한계를 확장하다', 즉 새로운 경지에 도달하거나 기존의 틀을 한 단계 넘어선다는 뜻입니다. 훨씬 더 창조적이라는 뜻이 되므로, 상업적이고 깊이가 없다는 말과는 반대죠.

정답 1.② 2.① 3.③ 4.② 5.④ 6.② 7.④ 8.① 9.①

세상을 말하는
스몰토크

SNS
뉴스
연예인
K-Drama
K-Pop
Exercise 4

SNS

139 페이스북 계정 있으세요? 페친합시다.

> Are you on Facebook? Let's be friends on Facebook.
>
> Do you have a Facebook profile? Let me send you a friend request.
>
> Can I find you on Facebook? I'd love to be Facebook friends.

'페이스북 계정이 있다'는 have a Facebook account라고 할 수 있지만, on Facebook이라고만 해도 페이스북을 활용하는 상태를 가리키므로 같은 의미가 됩니다. 페이스북 아이디나 계정은 두번째 문장처럼 Facebook profile이라고 말할 수도 있습니다.

> • 페이스북 계정이 있다
> on Facebook = have a Facebook profile

A Do you have a Facebook profile? Let me send you a friend request.
B Yeah, I do! I'm surprised we're not already connected on there.

A 페이스북 페이지 있으세요? 친구 요청을 보낼게요.
B 네 있어요. 아직 페이스북 친구 사이가 아니었다는 게 놀랍네요.

140 제 인스타 아이디는 @abc입니다. 놀러오세요.

My Instagram account is @abc. Please come visit sometime.

My Insta handle is @abc. Check it out if you can!

Here's my handle on Insta. I'd love it if you stopped by.

인스타그램을 '인스타(Insta)'라고 줄여 말하는 것은 영어도 마찬가지입니다. 두번째 문장처럼 handle이라고 해도 우리가 말하는 '인스타 아이디'에 해당하는 영어 표현입니다.

> • 인스타 아이디
> Instagram account = Insta handle = handle on Insta

A Do you use Instagram?
B Yeah, I do! What about you?
A I do too. My Insta handle is @abc. Check it out if you can!

A 인스타그램 하세요?
B 네, 하시나요?
A 네 저도요. 제 인스타 아이디는@abc입니다. 한번 들러 주세요.

SNS

141 틱톡 정말 좋아해요. 재미있는 동영상이 정말 많아요.

> I'm really into TikTok these days. There are a lot of fun videos.
>
> TikTok is my jam! The videos crack me up.
>
> TikTok is the best. The videos are hilarious.

hilarious는 fun, funny에서 더 나아가 큰 웃음을 유발하도록 웃기고 재미있는 것을 말합니다. 두번째 문장의 jam은 원래 음악에서 쓰이던 용어인데, 범위가 확대되어 재미있고 즐길 수 있는 것을 가리키는 속어가 되었습니다.

• **틱톡을 좋아하다**
be into TikTok = TikTok is my jam = TikTok is the best

• **동영상이 재미있다**
a lot of fun videos = crack me up = hilarious

A I'm really into TikTok these days. There are a lot of fun videos.
B Oh, same here! It's so addictive. What kind of videos do you usually watch?
A Mostly comedy skits and dance challenges. They always make me laugh.

A 요즘 틱톡에 빠져 있어요. 재밌는 영상이 정말 많아요.
B 저도요! 정말 중독성 있죠. 보통 어떤 영상을 보시나요?
A 주로 코미디나 댄스 챌린지요. 보면 항상 웃게 돼요.

142 소셜 미디어 너무 많이 안 하려고 합니다. 시간을 많이 뺏겨서요.

> I try not to visit social media sites so often. It sucks up too much of my time.
>
> I can't let myself visit social media too often. It's always a black hole of wasted time.
>
> I have to limit my social media time. I lose hours and hours through endless scrolling.

시간을 빨아들인다고 할 때 첫번째 문장처럼 suck up time이라고 말할 수 있습니다. 빨아들인다는 의미를 강조하기 위해 두번째 문장에서는 black hole을 활용하고 있죠. 세번째 문장의 endless scrolling은 화면을 계속 넘기는 행동을 표현합니다.

- **소셜 미디어를 많이 안 하다**
  not visit social media sites = not let myself visit social media
  = limit my social media time

- **시간을 많이 뺏어 간다**
  suck up too much of my time = a black hole of wasted time =
  lose hours and hours

A I try not to visit social media sites so often. It sucks up too much of my time.

B I get that. It's so easy to lose track of time scrolling through endless posts.

A 소셜 미디어 사이트를 자주 방문하지 않으려고 노력합니다. 시간을 너무 많이 잡아먹거든요.

B 이해가 가요. 계속 스크롤하다 보면 시간 가는 줄 모르게 되잖아요.

뉴스

143 최근 스포츠 관련 뉴스 뭐 있나요?

Can you **fill me in on** the latest sports news?

Can you **update me on** the latest sports news?

I'd like to **know what's new in** the world of sports.

fill me in은 직역하면 '나를 채워주다'인데, 어떤 '정보'를 알려주는 것을 가리킵니다. 두번째 문장의 update도 update me의 형태로 쓰면 '내게 새로운 정보를 업데이트해주다'라는 뜻이 되죠. 두 문장 모두 어떤 내용을 알려주는지는 전치사 on 다음에 넣어 표현하고 있습니다.

> • ~에 대해 알려주다
> fill me in on = update me on = know what's new in

A Can you fill me in on the latest of the World Cup?
B Sure! It's getting more interesting. Korea beat Brazil two to nil. It was definitely one of the upsets of the World Cup history.
A I can't believe I missed that. What happened next?

A 월드컵 관련 최신 뉴스 있으면 알려주시겠어요?
B 물론이죠. 점점 더 재미있어지고 있어요. 한국이 브라질을 2대 0으로 이겼어요. 월드컵 역사상 가장 큰 이변 중 하나였어요.
A 그런 경기를 놓치다니. 그리고 어떻게 되었어요?

144 처음 듣는 소식인데요.

That's news to me.

I haven't heard that before!

You're kidding! When did that happen?

'나에게는 새로운 뉴스다'라는 의미로 That's news to me.처럼 말하면 처음 듣는다는 의미가 되죠. 참고로 No new news.는 '새로운 소식이 없다'라는 뜻의 관용 표현입니다.

> • 처음 듣는 소식이다
> news to me = haven't heard before = when did that happen?

A Did you hear about the new policy they're implementing at work?
B No, I haven't. What is it?
A They're changing our work-from-home days to only one day a week instead of three.
B That's news to me. I guess we'll have to adjust our schedules then.

A 우리 회사 새 정책에 대해 들었어요?
B 아니요. 무슨 일인데요?
A 재택근무일을 주 3일에서 주 1일로 변경한대요.
B 전 몰랐어요. 그럼 일정을 조정해야 할 것 같네요.

뉴스

145 안 좋은 소식이 많아서 뉴스를 점점 덜 보게 되네요.

I get to watch less and less news programs on TV. There are so many bad stories.

I find myself watching fewer news programs on TV because there are so many negative stories.

I rarely watch the news on TV anymore. It's filled with too many bad stories.

내가 어떻게 한다고 말할 때, 두번째 문장처럼 '~하고 있는 자신을 발견한다(find)'라고 표현하는 경우가 많습니다. 세번째 문장에서는 rarely만을 활용해 '거의 ~하지 않는다'는 의미를 나타내고 있죠.

> • 뉴스를 덜 보다
> watch less and less news = watch fewer news = rarely watch the news
>
> • 안 좋은 소식
> bad stories = negative stories

A I find myself watching fewer news programs on TV because there are so many negative stories.
B I know what you mean. It can be tough to handle sometimes.
A Exactly. I try to stay informed, but it's hard when most of the news is so depressing.

A 저는 TV 뉴스를 덜 보게 됩니다. 부정적인 이야기가 너무 많거든요.
B 이해가 갑니다. 감당하기 힘든 때도 있잖아요.
A 맞아요. 정보를 놓치지 않으려 하지만, 우울한 뉴스 뿐일 때는 보기 힘들어요.

146 세상 돌아가는 걸 알기 위해 저녁 뉴스를 꼭 봅니다.

I try to watch prime-time news program every day to keep up with the way the world runs.

I make an effort to watch the prime-time news every day to stay informed about current events.

I make it a point to watch the prime-time news every day to stay in touch with how the world is running.

keep up with는 보조를 맞추거나 변화를 따라간다는 뜻입니다. stay informed 혹은 stay updated라고 하면, 정보를 얻거나(informed) 최신 상황에 대해 업데이트된 상태로 있다는 의미죠. stay in touch도 계속 접촉을 유지하며 변화에 적응한다는 뜻입니다.

> • 세상 돌아가는 걸 알다
> keep up with the way the world runs = stay informed about current events = stay in touch with how the world is running

A I try to watch prime-time news program every day to keep up with the way the world runs.
B Well, I find it hard to keep up with the news consistently.
A It can be tough, but it's important to stay informed about current events.

A 세상 돌아가는 거 따라가기 위해 매일 저녁 뉴스를 보려고 합니다.
B 글쎄요, 저는 계속 꾸준히 뉴스를 보는 게 힘들던데요.
A 힘들 수도 있지만, 시사에 대한 정보를 놓치지 않는 건 중요하죠.

연예인

147 김갑돌은 별로 좋아하는 사람도 없어 보이는데 TV에 왜 그리 많이 나오는 건가요?

> Kim doesn't seem to be liked by many people, so why does he appear on TV so often?
>
> Why is Kim frequently on TV when he isn't very popular with people?
>
> Why does Kim get so much TV airtime when he doesn't seem to have a lot of fans?

세번째 문장의 airtime은 말 그대로 방송(air)이 되는 시간(time)을 말합니다. 방송에 많이 나오는 것을 get so much airtime이라고 표현할 수 있죠.

- 좋아하는 사람이 없다
not liked by many people = not very popular = not have a lot of fans

- TV에 많이 나오다
appear on TV so often = be frequently on TV = get so much TV airtime

A Kim doesn't seem to be liked by many people, so why does he appear on TV so often?
B Yeah, I've noticed that too. I think it's because his controversy draws viewers.

A 김갑돌은 별로 인기가 없는 듯합니다. 그런데 왜 그렇게 TV에 자주 나오나요?
B 저도 그런 생각 했어요. 그가 일으키는 논란 때문에 시청자가 관심을 갖는 것 같아요.

148 예쁘고 지적이라서 김갑순의 팬입니다.

> I'm a big fan of Kim. She is pretty and looks very intelligent.
> I love Kim. She's gorgeous and looks really smart.
> I really like Kim. She's beautiful and very smart-looking.

얼굴을 포함한 외모가 훌륭하다고 할 때 두루 쓰는 단어가 gorgeous입니다. 지적인 모습은 smart와 intelligent를 활용하여 표현하면 되죠.

> **• 지적이다**
> look intelligent = look smart = smart-looking

A I'm a big fan of Sophia Bennett. She's gorgeous and looks really smart.
B I know. I watched her interview the other day, and she was very articulate and confident.
A Yeah, it's not just about looks. Her intelligence and charisma make her stand out even more.

A 저는 소피아 베넷의 열렬한 팬입니다. 아름답고 정말 똑똑해 보여요.
B 맞아요. 얼마 전 그녀의 인터뷰를 봤는데, 말을 잘 하고 자신감이 넘쳤어요.
A 네, 외모 때문만이 아니에요. 지성과 카리스마가 그녀를 더욱 돋보이게 해요.

연예인

149 유명해지는 것도 좋지만, 사생활이 없어지면 꼭 좋지만도 않을 것 같아요.

> Being a celebrity is fine, but it wouldn't be necessarily good if you lose your privacy.
>
> Being a celebrity sounds good, but it wouldn't be great if you lose your privacy.
>
> Being famous sounds nice, but it would be horrible if you lost your privacy.

celebrity는 유명인을 가리키는 가장 일반적인 단어입니다. '~도 좋지만 ~하다'는 ~ is fine/good/nice, but ~로 표현하면 됩니다.

- **~하는 것도 좋다**
  be fine = sound good = sound nice

- **좋지만도 않다**
  wouldn't be necessarily good = wouldn't be great = would be horrible

A Being a celebrity is fine, but it wouldn't be necessarily good if you lose your privacy.
B That's true. The constant attention must be stressful at times.
A Yeah, I can't imagine not being able to go anywhere without being recognized.

A 유명인이 되면 좋겠지만, 사생활이 없어진다면 꼭 좋은 건 아니겠죠.
B 그렇죠. 끊임없이 주목받는 건 때론 스트레스일 거예요.
A 맞아요. 어딜 가든 누군가 나를 알아본다는 건 상상도 못하겠어요.

150 김갑돌 좋아해요. 덕분에 나도 살을 빼려고 운동을 하게 되었어요.

I really like Kim. He inspired me to start my weight-loss journey.

I'm a big fan of his. He is the reason I started hitting the gym more.

I like Kim a lot. The way he lost so much weight really inspired me.

어떤 활동을 오래 지속하는 경우 여행에 빗대어 journey라고 표현하는 경우가 많습니다. hit the gym은 헬스클럽에 간다는 뜻이죠. hit the market(출시하다), hit the road(출발하다), hit the pillow(잠자다)처럼 hit을 활용해 어떤 동작이나 행위를 나타내는 표현들이 많습니다.

> • 나도 살을 빼기 시작하다
> start my weight-loss journey = start hitting the gym = the way he lost weight inspired me

A I really like Jason Ramirez. He inspired me to start my weight-loss journey.
B Yeah, I also think he made many people hit the gym more.
A He showed me that with hard work and persistence, I could achieve my goals too.

A 제이슨 라미레스 정말 좋아해요. 그는 제가 체중 감량을 시작하는 동기가 되었어요.
B 네, 저도 그 때문에 사람들이 헬스장에 더 자주 가게 되었다고 생각해요.
A 열심히 끈기 있게 노력하면 목표를 이룰 수 있다는 걸 깨닫게 해줬어요.

연예인

151 김갑순이 채식주의자라는데, 나도 한 번 해 볼까 합니다.

> I recently learned that Kim is a vegan, so I'm thinking of giving it a try.
>
> I heard that Kim is a vegetarian. I'm going to look up some vegetarian recipes later.
>
> I heard that Kim doesn't use any animal products, which makes me want to give it a go.

한번 시도해 보는 것을 give it a try/go/shot이라고 표현합니다. 보통 vegan이 vegetarian보다 더 엄격한데, 특히 동물을 활용한 음식이나 상품을 전혀 소비하지 않는 사람을 말합니다. 세번째 문장의 not use any animal products가 vegan의 특성에 해당하는 영어 표현이죠.

> • (채식주의자 되는 것을) 시도해 보다
> give it a try = look up vegetarian recipes = give it a go

A I recently learned that Mia Turner is vegan, so I'm thinking of giving it a try.
B Really? What made you decide that?
A Well, her lifestyle seems really healthy. I thought it might be a good way to improve my own eating habits.

A 미아 터너가 비건이라는 걸 최근에 알게 되었는데, 저도 시도해볼까 생각 중이에요.
B 정말요? 어떻게 그런 결정을 내리게 되었나요?
A 글쎄요, 그녀의 라이프스타일이 정말 건강해 보여서요. 제 식습관을 개선하는 좋은 방법이 될 것 같았어요.

152 김갑돌 이제 영화에 그만 나왔으면 좋겠어요.

I wish they would stop casting Kim.

I wish they'd stop giving Kim roles in movies.

I wish he'd stop showing up in movies.

cast는 캐스팅을 한다는 뜻이죠. 첫번째 문장은 '이제 그를 그만 캐스팅했으면 좋겠다'는 의미입니다. 결국 영화에 안 나오면 좋겠다는 말이 되죠.

> • 영화에 그만 나오다
> they stop casting him = they stop giving him roles in movies
> = he stops showing up in movies

A I wish they would stop casting Mark Wheeler.
B Really? What is it that you don't like about him?
A I just find his acting style so repetitive. It ruins the movies for me.
B I can see that. Sometimes it feels like he plays the same character in every film.

A 마크 휠러 이제 그만 캐스팅했으면 좋겠어요.
B 정말요? 어떤 점이 싫은데요?
A 그냥 연기 스타일이 너무 똑같아요. 제가 보기에는 영화를 망칩니다.
B 이해가 가요. 모든 영화에서 같은 캐릭터를 연기하는 것 같긴 해요.

연예인

153 김갑순이 컴백 앨범을 낸다던데, 그 사람 음악 좋아하세요?

> I heard Kim is making a comeback album. Do you like her music?
>
> I heard she's releasing a new album soon! Do you like her old stuff?
>
> I read that she's working on a comeback album. Are you a fan of hers?

음반이나 영화 등을 발표하는 경우 release로 표현할 수 있습니다. 세번째 문장의 work on은 추진하거나 노력하거나 애쓴다는 뜻으로 널리 쓰이는 구동사입니다. 다양한 경우에 활용해 보세요.

> **• 컴백 앨범을 내다**
> make a comeback album = release a new album = work on a comeback album

A I read that Lily Roberts is working on a comeback album. Are you a fan of hers?
B Yes, I've always loved her music. She has such a unique voice.
A Same here. I'm really excited to hear what she comes up with next.

A 릴리 로버츠가 컴백 앨범을 작업 중이라고 읽었어요. 팬이신가요?
B 네, 항상 릴리 로버츠 음악을 좋아했어요. 목소리가 정말 독특하죠.
A 저도요. 새롭게 무엇을 내놓을지 정말 기대돼요.

154 인스타그램으로 김갑순을 팔로우 하고 있어요.

I follow Kim on Instagram.

I'm one of Kim's Instagram followers.

I subscribe to Kim's posts on Instagram.

세번째 문장의 subscribe to는 구독한다는 뜻입니다. 소셜미디어 플랫폼에서 구독이나 팔로우를 나타낼 때 쓸 수 있는 표현이죠.

> • 인스타그램으로 팔로우하다
> follow her on Instagram = be one of her Instagram followers
> = subscribe to her posts on Instagram

A I follow Chloe Morgan on Instagram. I can't afford any of her products, though.
B Same here! I enjoy her posts and tips, and her lifestyle looks amazing, but those prices are way out of my league.

A 인스타그램으로 클로이 모건을 팔로우하고 있어요. 하지만 클로이 모건 제품은 못 사겠어요.
B 저도요! 클로이 모건의 게시글과 팁을 좋아하고, 라이프스타일도 정말 멋진 것 같지만, 제품의 가격은 감당 못하겠어요.

연예인

 페이스북으로 김갑순 팔로우 해봐요. 좋은 정보를 많이 올려요.

> You should follow Kim on Facebook because she's always posting great tips.
>
> You should find Kim on Facebook. She posts tons of great advice.
>
> You should add Kim on Facebook. She posts a lot on there, too.

인터넷이나 소셜 미디어에 뭔가를 올리는 것은 모두 동사 post로 표현하면 됩니다. 팔로우 하는 것은 follow 대신 add로 표현해도 좋죠.

> • 페이스북으로 팔로우하다
> follow her on Facebook = find her on Facebook = add her on Facebook

A Have you heard about Sarah's latest wellness tips?
B No, I haven't. Where can I find them?
A You should follow her on Facebook. She's always posting great tips.

A 건강에 대한 사라가 최근에 한 조언들 들어보셨나요?
B 아니요, 못 들어봤아요. 어디서 볼 수 있을까요?
A 페이스북에서 팔로우하세요. 항상 좋은 조언을 올려요.

유명인끼리 사귀는 얘기 많은데, 김갑돌이랑 이갑순이 오랫동안 몰래 사귀었다고 하네요.

> There are many rumors about celebrities seeing each other. Now people know that Kim and Lee were secretly in love for a long time.
>
> There are countless rumors about celebrities dating. Now, it's known that Kim and Lee had a long secret love.
>
> Many rumors circulate about celebrities' romantic lives. People now know that Kim and Lee had hidden their love for a long time.

첫번째 문장의 see는 단순히 본다는 뜻이 아니라, 남녀 간에 데이트를 한다는 의미입니다. 소문은 여기저기 돌아다니므로, 세번째 문장처럼 동사 circulate과 잘 어울립니다.

> **• 몰래 사귀다**
> be secretly in love = have a secret love = have hidden their love

A There are countless rumors about celebrities dating. Now, it's known that John Kim and Jane Lee had been secretly in love for a long time.
B Really? I always thought they were just good friends.
A 연예인끼리 사귀는 얘기 정말 많죠. 존 킴과 제인 리가 오랫동안 비밀리에 사귀었다고 알려졌어요.
B 정말요? 그냥 친한 친구 사이라고 생각했는데요.

K-Drama

157 한국 드라마는 감정의 과장이 심해요.

> Korean dramas are too melodramatic.
> Korean dramas are ridiculously dramatic.
> Korean dramas are too over-the-top.

감정적 요소나 극적 요소를 지나치게 강조하는 모양을 부정적으로 묘사하는 단어가 melodramatic입니다. 세번째 문장의 over-the-top도 과장되거나 지나치다는 뜻으로 쓰입니다. 1차 세계 대전에서 유래했는데, 참호 위로(over the top) 올라가는 것은 적의 기관총 공격에 노출되는 무모한 짓이었기 때문에 생겨난 표현이죠.

> • 감정의 과장이 심하다
> melodramatic = ridiculously dramatic = over-the-top

A Korean dramas are too melodramatic.
B I kind of agree. The storylines can be really over-the-top sometimes.
A True, but that's also what makes them so addictive for some people.

A 한국 드라마는 감정의 과장이 너무 심해요.
B 저도 어느 정도 동의해요. 줄거리가 가끔 말도 안 돼요.
A 그렇죠. 하지만 그래서 어떤 사람들에게는 중독성이 있기도 해요.

158 한국 드라마는 너무 뻔했는데, 요즘은 좀 변한 것 같습니다.

Korean dramas used to follow a predictable structure, but nowadays the writers are changing things up.

Korean dramas used to be very cookie-cutter, but these days they've gotten more individual.

Korean dramas used to be too similar, but recently I've noticed the writers are branching out into different directions.

음악, 영화, 드라마 등이 판에 박힌 듯 똑같을 때, 쿠키를 만드는 틀로 찍어 낸 것 같다는 의미에서 cookie-cutter라고 표현할 수 있습니다. 두번째 문장의 individual은 '개인적'보다는 '개별적' 혹은 '개성 있는'의 뜻으로 이해하면 됩니다.

> • 뻔하다
> predictable = cookie-cutter = too similar
>
> • 뻔하지 않게 바뀌다
> change things up = get more individual = branch out into different directions

A Korean dramas used to be very cookie-cutter, but these days they've gotten more individual.
B I know what you mean. The variety in storylines and character development is much better now.

A 한국 드라마 옛날에는 판에 박힌 듯했는데, 요즘은 다양해졌어요.
B 무슨 말인지 알겠어요. 줄거리와 캐릭터가 훨씬 발전했죠.

K-Drama

159 OTT 추천 목록에 한국 드라마들이 많아요. 전세계적으로 한국 드라마가 대세인 게 맞나봐요.

> There are many Korean dramas on the recommendation lists of OTT platforms. It seems true that Korean dramas are trending worldwide.
>
> Korean dramas are heavily featured on OTT recommendation lists. It's clear that Korean dramas are becoming a global sensation.
>
> OTT services are filled with Korean drama recommendations, reflecting their international appeal.

추천 목록에 한국 드라마가 많다고 할 때, 특징으로 한다고 번역되는 동사 feature를 활용할 수 있습니다. '대세'는 트렌드라는 뜻의 be trending, 센세이션을 일으킨다는 뜻의 sensation, 어필한다는 의미인 appeal로 표현하면 되죠.

• 추천 목록에 ~이 많다
many ~ on the recommendation lists = ~ are heavily featured on recommendation lists = be filled with ~ recommendations

• 전세계적으로 대세다
trending worldwide = a global sensation = international appeal

---

A Korean dramas are heavily featured on OTT recommendation lists. It's clear that Korean dramas are becoming a global sensation.
B Foreigners also seem to enjoy them. It's incredible how powerful culture can be.

A OTT 추천 목록에 한국 드라마가 많아요. 한국 드라마가 전 세계적으로 인기인 게 분명합니다.
B 외국에서도 한국 드라마를 좋아하더라고요. 문화의 힘이 대단한 것 같아요.

160 인물들이 매우 현실적이라서 내용이 꼭 실제 우리 생활 같아요.

The characters in the drama are so real that the show is more like our real life.

The characters on the show are so realistic that it's like they have cameras in my house.

The characters are so life-like that it's almost a case of holding a mirror up to society.

두번째 문장은 '마치 우리집을 카메라로 찍은 것처럼 리얼하다'라고 표현했죠. 세번째 문장에서 hold a mirror up to ~는 거울을 들이대서(hold up) 비친 모습을 그대로 보여주는 것처럼 리얼하다는 뜻입니다.

- 현실적이다
real = realistic = life-like

- 실생활 같다
be like our real life = like they have cameras in my house = hold a mirror up to society

A The characters in the drama are so real that the show is more like our real life.
B I know. It's amazing how they capture everyday situations so accurately.
A 드라마 속 캐릭터들이 너무 현실적이어서 마치 우리의 실제 삶 같아요.
B 그러게요. 일상에서 벌어지는 상황을 정확하게 포착한다는 점이 놀랍죠.

K-Drama

161 흥미로운 인물들은 많은데 그들의 생활이 현실적이지 않아요. 대부분의 한국인은 그렇게 살지 않습니다.

> There are many interesting characters, but their lives don't look real. Most Koreans don't live such a life.
>
> There are plenty of interesting characters, but they're all unrealistic. Most Koreans don't have that kind of lifestyle.
>
> The drama is packed with interesting people, but their lives are clearly fictional. Most Koreans lead totally different lives.

리얼하지 않은 것은 곧 허구와 같으므로, unrealistic, fictional과 같은 단어로 현실적이지 않음을 표현할 수 있습니다. 어떤 삶을 산다고 할 때 live a life 혹은 lead a life라고 하죠.

- **흥미로운 인물이 많다**
many interesting characters = plenty of interesting characters = packed with interesting people

- **그렇게 살지 않는다**
not live such a life = not have that kind of lifestyle = lead totally different lives

A There are plenty of interesting characters, but they're all unrealistic. Most Koreans don't have that kind of lifestyle.
B I agree. The dramas often portray the lifestyles that aren't really common.

A 재밌는 캐릭터는 많은데, 다 비현실적이에요. 대부분 한국 사람들은 그렇게 살지 않아요.
B 동의해요. 드라마는 일반적이지 않은 라이프스타일을 묘사하곤 하거든요.

162 그 드라마는 화목한 가정을 다루고 있어요. 그런 드라마 좋습니다.

> The drama deals with close relationships between family members. I like it.
>
> The drama follows intimate relationships between family members. It's my style.
>
> The main plotlines all revolve around family relationships. It's my cup of tea.

세번째 문장의 revolve around는 '~을 중심으로 회전한다'라고 직역할 수 있는데, 주제나 내용이 무엇에 중점을 두고 있는지 말할 때 쓰는 표현입니다.

- **화목한 가정**
close relationships between family members = intimate relationships between family members

- **그런 것을 좋아하다**
I like it = it's my style = it's my cup of tea

A The show deals with close relationships between family members. I like it.
B That sounds interesting. It's always nice to see strong family bonds portrayed on screen.
A Exactly. It makes the story more heart-warming.

A 그 드라마는 화목한 가정을 다루고 있어요. 그런 드라마 좋습니다.
B 재밌겠네요. 강한 유대감을 지닌 가족 이야기가 화면에 나오는 걸 보면 좋죠.
A 맞아요. 이야기가 더 따뜻해지죠.

K-Pop

163 케이팝은 다 너무 뻔하다고들 하는데, 노래가 귀에 쏙 들어오긴 하네요.

> I've heard K-pop is basically factory-made, but the songs are really catchy.
>
> I've been told that K-pop has no soul, but the songs are really fun to listen to.
>
> I've heard people complain that K-pop is very manufactured, but I like listening to the songs anyways.

예술가의 창조성이 발휘된 것이 아니라 마치 공장에서 만들어 낸 것 같다는 의미로 factory-made, manufactured와 같은 표현을 활용하고 있습니다. 첫번째 문장의 catchy는 귀에 쏙 들어오는 멜로디를 일컫는 단어입니다.

> • 뻔하다
> factory-made = has no soul = manufactured
>
> • 귀에 쏙 들어온다
> catchy = really fun to listen to = like listening to the songs

A I've heard K-pop is basically factory-made, but the songs are really catchy.
B Yeah, I've heard that too. The production quality is incredible though. They put so much effort into the music and choreography.

A 케이팝은 공장에서 만든 듯하다고들 하지만, 노래는 정말 중독성 있어요.
B 네, 저도 그런 말 들었어요. 제작 수준은 대단해요. 음악과 안무에 정말 많은 노력을 기울이죠.

164 케이팝 그룹들은 다 똑같이 보여요.

All the K-pop groups look alike to me!

I can't tell K-pop groups apart for the life of me!

When it comes to K-pop groups, I can't tell which is which.

두번째 문장의 for the life of me는 '내가 아무리 노력을 해도'라는 뜻입니다. 세번째 문장에서는 어떤 게 어떤 것인지 구분할 수가 없다는 의미로 can't tell which is which라는 표현을 활용했죠.

- **똑같아 보이다**
look alike = can't tell K-pop groups apart = can't tell which is which

A All the K-pop groups look alike to me!
B Really? I thought the same at first, but once you get to know them, you'll see they each have their own unique style.

A 전 모든 케이팝 그룹이 다 비슷해 보여요!
B 정말요? 저도 처음엔 그렇게 생각했는데, 케이팝을 알게 되면 각자만의 독특한 스타일이 있다는 걸 느낄 거예요.

K-Pop

165 케이팝 팬들은 좋아하는 그룹이나 가수에 대해 아주 열정적입니다.

K-pop fans are almost too passionate about their favorite groups or singers.

K-pop fans go hard for their preferred groups or singers.

Fans of K-pop are incredibly devoted to their chosen artists or groups.

열정적인 모습을 가리키는 형용사가 passionate이지만, go hard for ~라고 해도 ~에 대해 열정적이라는 뜻이 됩니다. 세번째 문장의 devoted는 헌신하는 모습을 가리키죠.

> • 매우 열정적이다
> be too passionate = go hard for = be incredibly devoted to

A K-pop fans are almost too passionate about their favorite groups or singers.
B Yeah, I think their dedication definitely helps the artists' popularity and success.

A 케이팝 팬들은 자신이 좋아하는 그룹이나 가수에 대해 너무 열정적이에요.
B 맞아요. 자신들의 헌신이 아티스트의 인기와 성공에 확실한 도움을 준다고 생각하죠.

166 한국 음악이 빌보드 차트 1위를 하다니, 저 어릴 때는 생각도 못한 일이에요.

> When I was young, I didn't even imagine there would come a time when Korean singers top the chart in Billboards.
>
> When I was little, I could never have guessed that someday Korean singers would top the Billboard chart.
>
> As a little kid, I never dreamed that someday I'd see Korean singers topping the US Billboard charts.

상상하거나(imagine) 꿈꾸거나(dream) 생각해 보는(guess) 것 모두 비슷한 의미를 지닌 동사들이죠. top을 동사로 활용해 top the chart라고 하면 차트 1위를 한다는 뜻입니다.

> • 언젠가 ~한 일이 일어나다
> there would come a time when = someday Korean singers would = someday I'd see

A When I was a kid, I never imagined that Korean singers would one day top the US charts.
B Yeah, it's incredible how global K-pop has become. BTS and BLACKPINK are everywhere now.

A 한국 가수들이 미국 차트 1위를 할 거라고는 제가 어렸을 때느 상상도 못했어요.
B 네, 케이팝이 얼마나 글로벌해졌는지 정말 놀랍죠. 지금은 어딜 가도 BTS와 블랙핑크예요.

K-Pop

167 케이팝이 한국에 대한 이미지를 좋게 만드는 것은 사실입니다.

> It's true that K-pop is creating positive images about Korea.
>
> Indeed, K-pop is creating a positive impression about Korea.
>
> That's right. K-pop is giving a good image of Korea to other countries.

좋은 이미지는 곧 좋은 인상이기도 하므로 image 대신 impression을 활용해도 좋습니다. 또, 이미지는 주는 것이기도 하니 give a good image도 자연스럽죠.

- **이미지를 좋게 만들다**
create positive images = create a positive impression = give a good image

A It's true that K-pop is creating positive images about Korea.
B Absolutely. It's amazing how it's become such a global phenomenon.
A It's not just the music, but also the culture and fashion that people are embracing.
B Yeah, K-pop has brought more interest in Korean language and traditions, too.

A 케이팝이 한국에 대한 긍정적인 이미지를 만드는 건 사실이에요.
B 물론이죠. 케이팝이 이렇게 세계적인 현상이 되었다니 정말 놀라워요.
A 사람들이 음악뿐 아니라 문화와 패션도 받아들이고 있어요.
B 네, 케이팝이 한국어와 한국의 전통에 대한 관심도 더 높였어요.

168 케이팝 스타들은 춤을 정말 잘 춰요. 가수들의 춤실력이 케이팝을 차별화하는 것 같습니다.

> K pop stars are very good at dancing. I think what differentiates K-pop from other genres of music is the singers' dance capabilities.
>
> K-pop singers are fantastic dancers. Their abilities set K-pop apart from other music genres.
>
> K-pop idols tend to be talented dancers. K-pop's choreography and moves put it in a league of its own.

'차별화'를 말할 때 우선 생각할 단어가 differentiate입니다. 차별화는 곧 자신을 구별하게 만드는 것을 의미하므로 두번째 문장처럼 set apart로 표현할 수도 있죠. 세번째 문장에서는 '자신만의 리그를 이루고 있다(in a league of its own)'이라고 했는데, 타인은 참여할 수 없는 리그를 가리키므로 그만큼 독보적이고 뛰어나다는 의미입니다.

- **춤을 잘 춘다**
  good at dancing = fantastic dancers = talented dancers

- **차별화하다**
  differentiate = set apart = put it in a league of its own

A K-pop stars are very good at dancing. I think what differentiates K-pop from other genres of music is the singers' dance capabilities.
B Absolutely. Their choreography is always so impressive and synchronized.

A 케이팝 스타들은 춤을 정말 잘 춰요. 케이팝을 다른 음악 장르와 차별화하는 건 가수들의 춤 실력이라고 생각해요.
B 물론이죠. 안무가 항상 멋지고 멤버들의 동작이 일치해요.

Exercise 4

다음 중 의미가 다른 문장 하나를 고르세요.

01

페이스북 계정 있으세요?

① Are you on Facebook?
② Are you disconnected from Facebook?
③ Do you have a Facebook profile?
④ Can I find you on Facebook?

02

소셜 미디어를 하면 시간을 많이 뺏겨요.

① Social media helps me make the most of my time.
② Social media sucks up too much of my time.
③ Social media is always a black hole of wasted time.
④ I lose hours and hours through endless scrolling on social media.

03

한국 드라마는 과장이 좀 심해요.

① Korean dramas are subtle and nuanced.
② Korean dramas are too melodramatic.
③ Korean dramas are ridiculously dramatic.
④ Korean dramas are too over-the-top.

04

세상 돌아가는 걸 알기 위해 저녁 뉴스를 꼭 봅니다.

① I try to watch prime time news program to keep up with the way the world runs.
② I avoid following the news to stay out of touch with reality.
③ I make an effort to watch the prime-time news to stay informed about current events.
④ I make it a point to watch the prime-time news to stay in touch with how the world is running.

05

그 사람 덕분에 나도 살을 빼려고 운동을 하게 되었어요.

① He inspired me to start my weight-loss journey.
② He is the reason I started hitting the gym more.
③ He cautioned me against losing weight.
④ The way he lost so much weight really inspired me.

06

한국 드라마는 너무 뻔했어요.

① Korean dramas used to follow a predictable structure.
② Korean dramas used to be original and diverse.
③ Korean dramas used to be very cookie-cutter.
④ Korean dramas used to be too similar.

07

인물들이 매우 현실적이어서 내용이 꼭 실제 우리 생활 같아요.

① The characters in the drama are so real that the show is more like our real life.
② The characters on the show are so realistic that it's like they have cameras in my house.
③ The characters are so life-like that it's almost a case of holding a mirror up to society.
④ The characters in the drama barely reflect anything about society.

08

케이팝은 노래가 귀에 쏙 들어오네요.

① K-pop songs are really catchy.
② K-pop songs are a lot of fun to listen to.
③ K-pop songs fail to grab attention.
④ K-pop songs are good to listen to.

09

가수들의 춤 실력이 케이팝을 차별화하는 것 같습니다.

① What differentiates K-pop from other genres of music is the singers' dance capabilities.
② The dancing abilities of K-pop singers take a backseat to what truly defines K-pop.
③ K-pop singers' abilities set K-pop apart from other music genres.
④ K-pop's choreography and moves put it in a league of its own.

Exercise 4 정답 및 해설

01
2번의 disconnect는 말 그대로 연결이 끊어진다는 뜻입니다. 페이스북 서비스를 이용하고 있다는 다른 문장들과는 반대 의미입니다.

02
1번의 make the most of one's time은 시간을 가장 잘 활용한다는 뜻이죠. '시간 낭비'와는 반대되는 의미입니다.

03
1번의 subtle과 nuanced는 모두 세밀하고 섬세한 차이가 느껴지도록 한다고 말할 때 쓰는 단어입니다. 특정 감정만 강조한다는 뜻인 나머지 세 문장과는 다르죠.

04
2번의 stay out of touch with reality는 현실과 동떨어진 모습을 가리키죠.

05
3번의 caution against ~는 ~하지 말라는 경고를 한다는 뜻입니다. 어떤 행동을 하라고 격려한다는 뜻인 나머지 세 문장과 반대됩니다.

06
2번의 original은 독창적인 모양을, diverse는 다양한 모습을 일컫습니다. 뻔하다는 의미와는 거리가 멀죠.

07
4번의 reflect는 반영한다는 뜻인데, barely와 함께 썼으므로 '거의 반영하지 않는다'라는 의미입니다. '현실을 거의 반영하지 못한다'는 말이므로 4번이 정답입니다.

08

3번의 grab attention은 주의를 끈다는 뜻인데, fail to가 붙어 그러하지 못한다는 의미가 되므로, 나머지 문장들과 다릅니다.

09

2번의 take a backseat to는 '뒷좌석을 차지한다', 즉 뒷전으로 밀린다는 뜻입니다. 춤 실력이 첫번째 요인이라는 다른 문장들과 달리, 첫번째 요인이 되지 못한다고 말하고 있으므로 답은 2번입니다.

정답 1.② 2.① 3.① 4.② 5.③ 6.② 7.④ 8.③ 9.②